D0559367

To Sow One Acre More

The Johns Hopkins University
Studies in Historical and Political Science
111th Series (1993)

1. *To Sow One Acre More: Childbearing and
Farm Productivity in the Antebellum North*
by Lee A. Craig

To Sow One Acre More

CHILDBEARING AND FARM PRODUCTIVITY
IN THE ANTEBELLUM NORTH

Lee A. Craig

The Johns Hopkins University Press
Baltimore and London

The Johns Hopkins University Press
2715 North Charles Street
Baltimore, Maryland 21218-4319
The Johns Hopkins Press Ltd., London

Library of Congress Cataloging-in-Publication Data

Craig, Lee A. (Lee Allan), 1960–
    To sow one acre more : childbearing and farm productivity in the
antebellum north / Lee A. Craig.
        p.   cm. — (The Johns Hopkins University studies in historical
and political science ; 111th ser., 1)
    Includes bibliographical references and index.
    ISBN 0-8018-4529-7 (acid-free paper)
    1. Fertility, Human—Economic aspects—United States—History—
19th century.   2. Family farms—United States—History—19th
century.   3. Rural children—Employment—United States—History—
19th century.   4. Rural families—United States—History—19th
century.   5. Agricultural productivity—United States—History—19th
century.   I. Title.   II. Series.
HB915.C7   1993
338.1′4—dc20   92-40483

A catalog record for this book is available from the British Library.

To My Parents

Contents

Preface and Acknowledgments

This book examines the household economy—the commonplace decisions that decided a family's fortunes—in the northern countryside on the eve of the Civil War, explaining changes in rural American life that reverberate to this day. One of the most striking changes in family life over the past two hundred years has been the decline in the number of children. Between the founding of the republic and 1900, the crude birthrate in the United States fell by almost one-half, from more than fifty live births per thousand human population to less than thirty. (Today it stands at sixteen.) Birthrates varied considerably among geographical regions as well as over time. A large measure of the fall in nineteenth-century birthrates resulted from changes in childbearing patterns in rural areas. Families in newer states generally experienced higher fertility rates, often 50 percent higher or more, than those in older, more settled regions, and rural birth rates exceeded those of urban areas by about the same degree. Why did rural fertility rates fall? Why did they fall in more settled regions first?

To answer these questions we must draw a clear picture of the economics of the farm household, focusing on the northern states from Maine to Kansas during the early nineteenth century. Reproduction is perhaps the most fundamental aspect of an organism's existence, and within a relatively short period of time in the nineteenth century, almost every developed country in the world experienced a transition from high to low fertility rates, the causes and consequences of which social scientists still debate. Estimating the economic value of children places these changes in fertility in an analytical framework that may answer questions about the decline and regional pattern of birthrates in the antebellum North and indeed throughout the Western world during the past two centuries.

The evidence strongly suggests that the regional character of the decline in rural birthrates was inextricably linked to diminished access to inexpensive farm land and changes in agricultural markets and technology. Thomas Jefferson believed the freeholding system, in which individual families owned and operated their farms, supplied the bedrock of economic democracy. He considered that disposing of the public domain in a manner encouraging to a yeomanry was one of the most important tasks facing the new republic. Access to inexpensive land drove the Jeffersonian system, and the course of economic history sealed the fate of Jeffersonian agrarianism. In most regions, after a short period of initial settlement, birthrates rose, but as inexpensive land became more difficult to obtain, birthrates invariably fell. Yet neither modernization nor population density drove birthrates downward by themselves. Rather, the opportunities offered by industry and the western frontier, changes in how parents and children exchanged income and wealth, and the evolution of agricultural technology and markets all contributed to lower birthrates in rural communities. Although this book analyzes many features of farm households, an interest in a broader understanding and explanation of that most intimate of household decisions, childbearing (and thus fertility rates), pervades every chapter.

No matter what approach one takes toward addressing these questions—the neoclassical marginalism of traditional economics, the game theory of the "new institutional" economics, or the class conflict of Marxian economics—one cannot avoid either the explicit or implicit calculation of the economic value of children. Some readers, particularly those trained in the humanities, may shrink from that phrase, as if I mean to imply that nineteenth-century farmers decided to have children the way capitalists figure how many workers to hire. Such a response wrongly supposes that economics is incapable of recognizing the psychic rewards of bearing and raising children and implies that the discipline lacks humanity. Yet if the dismal scientists themselves lack humanity, economics does not. I take the term *economic value of children* to mean, in the broadest sense, their value as producers and contributors to real household output, as "consumption goods"— that is as providers of pride and satisfaction to their parents—and as potential sources of security, both economic and emotional, for parents in their declining years.

Calculating the productive value of children may seem absurd today, when children seldom contribute more to the household than taking out the garbage or keeping their rooms clean. In the nineteenth century, however, parents expected children to pitch in on the farm along with the rest of the family, and a farm couple without children carried a heavy burden. "Lo, children are a heritage of the Lord: and the fruit of the womb is his reward," read Psalm 127 in the Bible that virtually every nineteenth-century American farmer kept prominently in the house. "As arrows are in the hand of a mighty man; so are children of the youth. Happy is the man that hath a quiver full of them" (Psalm 127:3–5). But how much did children contribute to the farm economy? How did their contribution change as they grew up? Was there a difference between the contributions of males and females? Did the value of children differ between regions and, if so, why? After children were born, did parents adjust the farm operation to take advantage of the differences in the human capital embodied in children of different ages? How did the net value of a child in northern agriculture differ from that of a slave child? How did the role of women in the farm economy affect fertility? Did these roles differ among regions? This book answers these questions.

These questions and much of the methodology employed to address them stem from a discussion I had with Marvin McInnis while strolling through the grounds at Allerton House in Monticello, Illinois, at the 1987 Cliometrics Society Meetings. Among the economists, demographers, historians, and sociologists who had studied the decline in nineteenth-century birthrates in rural America, McInnis represented the minority view that children were more valuable in the more settled regions of the Northeast, while the majority argued that the frontier provided the greatest opportunity for the employment of children. During our conversation Professor McInnis pointed out that none of the scholars involved in the debate had directly estimated the value of farm children among different regions. Since I had in my possession the Bateman-Foust sample of more than 20,000 rural households from the 1860 census,[1] he suggested I use it to test various hypotheses concerning the economic value of children and the relationship between the value of children and regional birthrates. This book represents the result, with numerous additions, of that suggestion.

As with any volume of this type, many individuals deserve much credit, though none of the blame, for the final version. Phil Coelho must take the responsibility for stimulating my initial curiosity about population change and the emergence of industrial economies from agrarian roots. George Alter, Fred Bateman, R. Jeffery Green, Elyce Rotella, and George Stolnitz all influenced this work through their guidance both in and out of the classroom. Elyce Rotella provided advice, persuasion, criticism, guidance, and friendship in what seems in retrospect like just the right quantities at just the right times. My association with her is among the most valued of the many rewards I received from a graduate education. Jeremy Atack reviewed the manuscript in its entirety, supplying many helpful comments, as did Tom Weiss on several occasions. Robert J. Brugger at the Johns Hopkins University Press provided many thoughtful suggestions, as did an anonymous reviewer, and Lys Ann Shore edited the manuscript. Special thanks are due to my colleagues at North Carolina State University, Douglas Fisher and V. Kerry Smith, without whose encouragement, suggestions, and advice this book would never have been published.

I prepared the final manuscript while on leave at the Center for Demographic Studies at Duke University. I thank the director, George Myers, for the opportunity to continue my research at the center. Portions of this book have been presented in various forms at seminars at the University of Chicago, the University of Illinois, Indiana University, Northwestern University, the Triangle University Economic History Workshop, and the annual meetings of the Economic History Association and the Social Science History Association. I collectively thank the participants, who are too numerous to name individually. In addition, the Graduate School at Indiana University provided partial funding for the collection of the data.

Special thanks go to my wife, Jackie, for her unending patience in sharing with me the vagaries of academic life. Finally, I dedicate this book to my parents. It serves as confirmation that the examples of hard work and dedication they provided in my youth were not lost on me, and its completion is as much their accomplishment as my own.

To Sow One Acre More

CHAPTER ONE

The Decline of Rural Birthrates in the Antebellum North

In his reflections on antebellum American society, Alexis de Tocqueville described the nation as offering unparalleled egalitarianism, particularly in rural areas of the Old Northwest: Ohio, Indiana, Illinois, Michigan, and Wisconsin. "States whose names were not in existence a few years before claimed their place in the American Union; and in the Western settlements we may behold democracy arrived at its utmost extreme. In these States, founded offhand, and, as it were, by chance, the inhabitants are but of yesterday. Scarcely known to one another, the nearest neighbors are ignorant of each other's history. In this part of the American continent, therefore, the population has not experienced the influence of great names and great wealth."[1]

By today's standards, Tocqueville's observations of the United States in the 1830s seem hopelessly naive and Eurocentric. Given the unequal distribution of wealth and political power in the nineteenth century, they appear inaccurate as well. Yet before rejecting the notion of antebellum America as a land of equality, one must ask, "Compared to what?" By 1860, the distribution of wealth in urban areas looked much as it has in recent decades; the richest 1 percent of the population controlled more than a quarter of the total wealth. But in rural areas of the North, the richest 1 percent owned only about 12 percent of the wealth. Compared to the traveler's native France, Europe, or the rest of the United States, rural dwellers in the antebellum North enjoyed a distinctly equitable distribution of wealth. The distribution of wealth among northern farmers was more equal than for any other group in antebellum America, rural or urban, North or South, and property in

1

the Midwest was distributed more equally than in either England or France at the time.[2] The rural North truly represented a land of equality, "the best poor man's country" in the world.[3]

Thomas Jefferson—according to Tocqueville America's greatest democrat—envisioned the nation as a land of yeomen farmers, men and women of the soil who owned and operated their own farms, citizens who provided subsistence for themselves and their families and a surplus for export to and consumption by the necessary few artisans and merchants in urban areas. Like Cicero, who said that of all occupations agriculture represented the finest and that there was "nothing more worthy of a freeman,"[4] Jefferson thought agriculture the economic manifestation of democratic virtues. "The small landowners are the most precious part of the State," wrote Jefferson, reflecting on the unequal distribution of wealth he had witnessed in rural France and on its portents for democracy there.[5] Although the Industrial Revolution ultimately doomed Jefferson's Arcadia, the rural economy of the antebellum North was as close as America and the Western world would come to that agrarian vision.

These yeomen, refugees or descendants of refugees from a feudal heritage, settled a vast and largely unpopulated country. They brought its land into production under institutional arrangements that would have made the squires, boyars, and junkers of the Old World blanch. Land tenure in the new republic excluded many of the features that marked land tenure in Europe. Quitrents (payments in lieu of labor dues), escheat (the reversion of land to the lord or crown), and mortmain (no right of alienation) maintained no place in American land tenure.

Not everyone who came shared in the relative political and economic freedom of the new land—the 4 million blacks who were in bondage by 1860 being the most obvious example. Nor did women receive an equal share of either economic wealth or political power. Within the household, and especially outside it, women had access to fewer economic opportunities than men. Harriet Martineau, who traveled through the North in 1834–35 and whose views seem in retrospect more balanced than Tocqueville's, claimed that "indulgence is given [woman] as a substitute for justice. Her case differs from that of the slave, as to the principle, just so far as this; that the indulgence is large and universal, instead of petty and capricious."[6] Despite these injustices, many of which occurred within the household, the distribution of wealth among rural northern households remained equal by historical standards.

For a century or more after the United States won its independence from Britain, the establishment of farms on the trans-Appalachian frontier proceeded along well-defined lines. Once an agreement, coerced or negotiated, had been established with the Native Americans (and often before), the Land Office sectioned the countryside by celestial survey, and agents sold at auction the fertile acreage of the Old Northwest and beyond. The Land Ordinance of 1785, passed under the Articles of Confederation, established the initial minimum purchase of 640 acres (one square mile) at a minimum or reservation price of $1 an acre. The Land Act of 1796 raised the reservation price to $2 an acre, but with the ascendance of the Jeffersonians and the continuing westward shift of the axis of power in national politics, the terms under which one could acquire land eased. The Cash Sale Act of 1820 established the reservation price of public land at $1.25 an acre and reduced the minimum purchase to 80 acres. The Land Act of 1832 further reduced the minimum purchase to 40 acres, and subsequent legislation, such as the Preemption (Squatter's) Act of 1841 and the Graduation Act of 1854, made farm ownership even more accessible. The act of 1841 broadly recognized squatting—apparently a time-honored Western tradition, since the term comes from feudal land tenure—by allowing a family to preempt up to 160 acres at the reservation price. The act of 1854 provided for the sale of previously auctioned but unsold land at prices below the reservation price, with land that went unsold for thirty years available for 12 1/2¢ an acre. Further, the land warrants Congress issued to veterans of the antebellum military campaigns typically circulated at prices below the reservation price, often at around 75¢ an acre. Although the much maligned land "speculators"—according to one antebellum writer "a withering blight of influence"[7]—often purchased large tracts to be divided and resold with a markup, by the late antebellum period, $30–$50, the equivalent of one and a half to two months' pay without board for a hired farmhand, could secure the deed to 40 acres of the public domain in the northern Mississippi Valley.

In 1860 more than half of all Americans lived on farms, and agriculture employed two-thirds of the labor force in the Old Northwest. The original American dream was to acquire enough land to support a farm family, and inexpensive land became an essential part of western expansion. The vast majority of northern farmers owned all the land they farmed, and a significant proportion rented still more. Only 10 percent of northern farmers owned no land at all, but this group included many young families starting on a low rung of an agricultural ladder that would eventually take them to ownership. It became apparent soon after the land sales began that even small-scale farmers could purchase more land than they immediately required to support a family, with the intention of clearing or selling the remainder as the family situation and market conditions dictated. The trans-Appalachian Northwest offered great tracts of fertile land that could be purchased in blocks and resold as prices rose, and speculating in the public lands soon became a major industry. "A little money judiciously invested here will be placed at good interest," one Iowa speculator wrote to a colleague back East. "I am much pleased with the country [and] all my savings I invest in the soil."[8] This interest in land for investment purposes stemmed from the large role agriculture played in the antebellum economy, and the availability of more land at lower prices induced a westward shift of resources, namely, farm families and the capital they brought with them.

Although the population of the entire country grew rapidly by historical standards, birthrates in the United States, as well as in most of the countries of western Europe, declined throughout the nineteenth century. The free population of the early republic experienced crude birthrates of fifty or higher. (The *crude birthrate* is the number of live births per thousand total population.) Crude birthrates that high have rarely occurred in the Western world since the eighteenth century. The biological maximum (or noncontracepting "natural") fertility rate of Homo sapiens has been estimated at around sixty per thousand. By the end of the nineteenth century, crude birthrates had dropped to below thirty, and by the 1980s they had sunk to around sixteen. Differences existed between the birthrates in various regions of the country probably as early as colonial times. As a result of the western migration and the almost invariably higher birthrates in rural areas, the predominantly rural Old Northwest and trans-Mississippi frontier experienced higher rates of population growth than the more settled areas in the Northeast. By 1860, women on midwestern farms gave birth on average to 50 percent more children than women on northeastern farms.[9]

In the eighteenth century Adam Smith—a Scottish professor of moral philosophy, father of the discipline of economics, and a man who missed little when it came to observing the socioeconomic scene of his day—speculated that a relationship between the ease of access to land and population growth marked the American colonies. Shortly thereafter, Thomas Malthus, a Cambridge-educated Anglican parson, constructed a theory of population growth in which birthrates ultimately fell as the population in a particular region pressed against the

4

means of subsistence. A half century later, Tocqueville and others recognized that the regional populations of the United States were growing at different rates. Tocqueville noted that the Mississippi Valley was "far more fertile than the coast of the Atlantic Ocean. This reason, added to all the others, contributes to drive the Europeans westward— a fact which may be rigorously demonstrated by figures. It is found that the sum total of the population of all the United States has about trebled in the course of forty years. But in the recent States adjacent to the Mississippi the population has increased thirty-one fold within the same space of time."[10]

Western migration no doubt contributed much to this sudden population growth, but by the middle of the nineteenth century regional birthrates displayed relatively large differences as well. Ezra Seaman and George Tucker, both antebellum American political economists, separately recognized the large proportion of the population under ten years of age in the Mississippi valley relative to the Atlantic seaboard and also the falling birthrates in the more settled part of the country. Seaman commented on the implications of these demographic changes for regional population growth; recognizing the direct relationship between birthrates and population density, Tucker noted that "the natural increase of the population is inversely as its density; and this is apparent, whether we compare the increase of the same State at different periods, or the increase of one State or one division with another."[11]

After 1830 one-half to two-thirds of the population growth in the United States came from areas that were not part of the country in 1790, and by 1880 more than half of the total population resided in these new areas (table 1.1). The rates of population growth in the Mississippi Valley exceeded those of the Northeast throughout the century. Throughout the nineteenth century the *child-woman ratio*— that is, the number of children under five years old per thousand white women age twenty to forty-four—increased from east to west (table 1.2). The higher birthrates in less settled areas, recognized by Seaman and Tucker, show up in the high child-woman ratios in those regions.

Because the West was predominantly rural, and because rural populations displayed higher fertility than urban populations, it follows that East-West differences in birthrates could have been explained at least partly by the differences in the proportion of the population that lived in rural areas. But contemporary commentators and early scholars did not conduct direct comparisons between fertility rates in the *rural* East and the *rural* West. Such a comparison of birthrates reveals that rates in the western states exceeded those of the eastern states as early

5

Table 1.1 Percentage Increase in Population from Preceding Census

Year	United States	New England	Middle Atlantic	East North-Central	West North-Central
1800	34.8%	22.2%	46.3%	—	—
1810	36.4	19.4	43.6	435.9%	—
1820	33.1	12.8	34.0	191.1	236.6%
1830	34.1	17.7	32.9	85.4	110.9
1840	32.7	14.3	26.2	99.0	203.9
1850	35.9	22.1	30.3	54.7	106.3
1860	35.5	14.9	26.5	53.1	146.5
1870	26.6	11.2	18.1	31.7	77.7
1880	25.9	15.0	19.1	22.8	59.7
1890	25.4	17.2	21.0	20.3	45.1

Sources: Warren S. Thompson and P. K. Whelpton, *Population Trends in the United States* (New York: McGraw-Hill, 1933); Conrad Taeuber and Irene B. Taeuber, *The Changing Population of the United States* (New York: John Wiley and Sons, 1958); U.S. Commerce Department, *Historical Statistics of the U.S., Colonial Times to 1970* (Washington, D.C.: Government Printing Office, 1975).

Note: Regions are defined as follows: *New England*—Maine, New Hampshire, Vermont, Massachusetts, Rhode Island, and Connecticut; *Middle Atlantic*—New York, New Jersey, and Pennsylvania; *East North-Central*—Ohio, Indiana, Illinois, Michigan, and Wisconsin; *West North-Central*—Minnesota, Iowa, Missouri, Dakota, Nebraska, and Kansas.

Table 1.2 Number of Children under 5 Years Old per 1,000 White Women 20–44 Years Old

Year	United States	New England	Middle Atlantic	East North-Central	West North-Central
1800	1,342	1,164	1,334	1,918	—
1810	1,358	1,111	1,365	1,777	1,915
1820	1,295	980	1,244	1,683	1,768
1830	1,145	826	1,044	1,473	1,685
1840	1,085	770	951	1,280	1,446
1850[a]	892	636	776	1,037	1,122
1860[a]	905	639	784	1,016	1,118
1870[a]	814	564	702	892	1,012
1880[a]	780	520	648	781	930
1890[a]	685	456	563	668	797

Sources: Thompson and Whelpton, *Population Trends*; Taeuber and Taeuber, *Changing Population*; and Commerce Department, *Historical Statistics*.

Note: Regions are defined as follows: *New England*—Maine, New Hampshire, Vermont, Massachusetts, Rhode Island, and Connecticut; *Middle Atlantic*—New York, New Jersey, and Pennsylvania; *East North-Central*—Ohio, Indiana, Illinois, Michigan, and Wisconsin; *West North-Central*—Minnesota, Iowa, Missouri, Dakota, Nebraska, and Kansas.

[a] Includes black women.

as 1800, and the rural populations of the states on or just behind the frontier maintained the highest crude birthrates throughout the antebellum era (table 1.3).[12] At the turn of the century, rural families in the Ohio and Indiana territories had the highest birthrates; by the 1830s, Michigan and Wisconsin led the way; and by the end of the era the most prolific producers of children lived in the Plains states: Kansas, Nebraska, Minnesota, and the Dakotas.

Pioneering studies of nineteenth-century childbearing that attempted to explain this behavior yielded two major findings. First, they

Table 1.3 Ranking from Highest to Lowest of States and Territories by Crude Birthrate, 1790–1860

	1790–1800	1800–1810	1810–20	1820–30	1830–40	1840–50	1850–60
New England							
Maine	4	5	6	8	9	12	13
New Hampshire	7	9	11	12	12	15	16
Vermont	5	7	9	10	11	14	16
Massachusetts	9	10	10	11	10	13	15
Rhode Island	10	11	12	13	13	13	14
Connecticut	8	8	8	9	9	10	11
Middle Atlantic							
New York	2	4	5	7	8	11	12
New Jersey	6	6	7	6	7	8	9
Pennsylvania	3	3	4	5	5	7	8
East North-Central							
Ohio[a]	1	2	3	4	6	9	10
Indiana[a]	1	1	1	3	4	6	7
Illinois[a]	—	1	1	2	3	5	6
Michigan[a]	—	1	2	1	2	3	4
Wisconsin[a]	—	—	—	—	1	2	3
West North-Central							
Minnesota[a]	—	—	—	—	—	1	1
Iowa[a]	—	—	—	—	1	2	2
Missouri[a]	—	—	1	2	3	4	5
Dakotas	—	—	—	—	—	—	1
Nebraska	—	—	—	—	—	—	1
Kansas	—	—	—	—	—	—	1
Weighted mean	54.1	52.4	52.6	50.9	47.0	44.0	41.4

Source: Author's calculation from Morton Schapiro, "Land Availability and Fertility in the United States, 1760–1870," *Journal of Economic History* 42 (September 1982): 577–600.

[a]States underwent territorial changes that may make comparisons across census years misleading.

confirmed the hypotheses of contemporaries that rural populations in regions with easily obtainable land maintained higher birthrates than those in more settled rural areas. Since land was generally more easily obtained the farther west one went, this observation became a focal point of explanations of the East-West gradient in rural fertility rates that persisted throughout the first century or so of U.S. history. As part of President Herbert Hoover's Research Committee on Social Trends, Warren Thompson and P. K. Whelpton published *Population Trends in the United States*, in which they documented the rapid growth of population in newer regions throughout U.S. history. Thompson and Whelpton attributed this phenomenon to the opportunity offered by the inexpensive fertile land available on the frontier. Second, studies revealed that industrialization and urbanization did not play a direct role in determining fertility until the middle of the nineteenth century. After that time, however, industrial and urban growth may well have surpassed the availability of land as explanatory factors. Agriculture remained the primary economic pursuit of the American people in the first half of the century. For example, the *value added*—the value of output or total revenue less the value of raw material and intermediate goods—in the industrial sector did not surpass that of agriculture until the 1880s, and not until after World War I did manufacturing employment exceed agricultural employment. So theories of early fertility decline must explain the decline of rural fertility even after accounting for the effects of industrialization.

Almost every Western nation experienced a dramatic decline in rates of reproduction, known as the *fertility transition*, during the late nineteenth century. Significantly, this decline began earlier in the United States than in most of Europe. The child-woman ratio for the country as a whole fell by more than 30 percent, and the crude birthrate fell by almost 25 percent in rural areas of the North between 1800 and 1860 (tables 1.2 and 1.3). In addition, the *total fertility rate*—that is, the number of live births a woman could expect to have given current age-specific birthrates—fell by 26 percent for the country as a whole, from 7.04 in 1800 to 5.21 in 1860.[13] Among European countries, only France experienced comparable declines that early. This difference in timing, together with the discovery of regional differences in birthrates in the United States, indicates that the social and economic changes that affected fertility decline in America probably differed from those ascribed to fertility decline in Europe and elsewhere as a result of the "rapidity of . . . modernization accompanying industrialization."[14] The United States was not an industrial nation when rapid fertility decline began, and numerous examples exist of fertility behavior being related to population density in general and to access to inexpensive farm land in particular.

Studies of Madison County, New York, show that the decline in fertility began early in the nineteenth century, and that fertility of farm families probably fell before that of urban families. Furthermore, in the entire state of New York between 1840 and 1875, both urban and rural birthrates fell, but rural rates fell faster. In both cases a significant negative correlation existed between population density and the average number of children a woman ever gave birth to; this was true for native-born and foreign-born white women. In other words, by the middle of the nineteenth century birthrates began to fall in northeastern agricultural communities at the same time as, if not before, those in urban areas, they fell more rapidly in rural areas, and their decline was highly correlated with an increase in relative land scarcity.[15]

An increase in relative land scarcity in agricultural communities often constituted a form of "economic stress." The scholarly quest for quantification of economic stress resulted in the construction of a measure based on the extent of the excess supply (an absence of stress) or excess demand (the presence of stress) for farm sites in the antebellum North.[16] A study testing the relationship between this measure and the birthrate for Ohio counties between 1850 and 1860 found that economic stress adversely affected fertility, but it found no effect on the birthrate from the proportion of the population in urban areas. In other words, land availability and not urbanization explained fertility rates, corroborating the view that modernization can not explain the onset of the fertility transition in rural America, at least to the extent that measures of urbanization and industrialization represent modernization.[17]

Another study employed the same measure of economic stress in conjunction with other economic and social variables to explain antebellum northern fertility. The study included the percentage of households operating farms in a given township. This variable reflected changes in the demand for child labor on farms and increased opportunity for women off farms. Other variables included the percentage of the population with New England roots, the percentage of Irish and German immigrants, and the percentage of other immigrants. These variables attempted to capture cultural effects, and a wealth variable was included as well. The results suggested that land pressure, wealth, and proportion of the population from New England all significantly reduced the child-woman ratio. Conversely, the percentage of households on farms and the percentage of households from immigrant

9

groups other than Irish and German all significantly increased the child-woman ratio.[18] So land pressure had a negative effect on fertility rates, but urbanization probably had a negative effect as well.

Other measures of land pressure have been used to explain the fertility of northern farm families. For example, the ratio of the rural population of a state at a given time to its maximum rural population ever reached also had a strong and significant negative effect on the child-woman ratio.[19] Because of the role of land pressure in the determination of fertility rates in these studies, they have been called "Malthusian," after the parson who predicted the decline of birthrates due to increasing population density. Collectively, the studies further documented the positive relationship between land scarcity and birthrates originally postulated by Smith, Malthus, and others, but they failed to offer an explanation of the mechanism through which population density affected birthrates. In the words of Colin Forster and G. S. L. Tucker, "there does seem to have been a meaningful socioeconomic relation between [birthrates] and the abundance or scarcity of opportunities near to the place of residence for the establishment of new farms, and this may help to account both for the height of American fertility at the beginning of the nineteenth century and its subsequent downward trend."[20] This conclusion supports earlier studies and the observations of contemporaries, but it does not, nor did they, offer an explicit theory of why or how the ratio of population to farm land explains fertility differences over time or space.[21] Explaining the fertility transition in nonindustrial economies like that of the antebellum United States contributes not only to historical research but also to the study of childbearing in contemporary developing countries. The studies of this topic just reviewed, however, focused on obtaining empirical results and described rather than explained fertility behavior. They left considerable room for further analysis.

The evidence presented so far shows that population density fell and fertility rates rose as one went from east to west across the northern half of nineteenth-century America. But what constituted the Northeast or Northwest? One way to avoid the problems of definition would be to proceed by state, as in table 1.3. States are political units, however, not economic or social ones. To preserve a coherent economic and geographic division of farms, I have divided the North into three regions: Northeast, Midwest, and Frontier. Townships in the states of Connecticut, New Hampshire, New Jersey, New York, Pennsylvania, and Vermont composed the Northeast; those in Illinois, Indiana, Ohio, and southern Michigan and Wisconsin made up the Midwest; and those in Iowa, Kansas, Minnesota, and northern Michigan and Wisconsin constituted the Frontier. Whether a farm fell into a particular region depended on the extent of settlement in that farm's township. Although there are any number of ways of dividing up the northern farms, this division of households corresponds roughly to the extent of rural settlement in 1860. The primary data set employed in this study is the one constructed by Fred Bateman and James Foust in 1974 from a matched sample of more than 20,000 rural households, more than half of which were farm households, located in 102 townships across the North. They drew this sample from the 1860 censuses of agriculture and population.

Most previous studies employed the child-woman ratio as their measure of fertility. But the child-woman ratio and the crude birthrate can be heavily influenced by differences in the age structure of the population; younger populations tend to have higher child-woman ratios and higher crude birthrates. For this reason, the total fertility rate makes a better measure in some instances.[22] Employing this measure to determine differences between the fertility rates of farm women in the Northeast and those in the Midwest and on the Frontier yields a total fertility rate in 1860 of 4.54 for the Northeast and 6.66 for the Midwest and Frontier combined.[23] So the average farm woman in Indiana or Illinois could expect to give birth to almost half again as many children as her counterpart in New York or Vermont. Differences in the components of the total fertility rate show that the ratio of men to women must have been higher in the Midwest and on the Frontier than in the Northeast. For example, the proportion of women who married accounted for the largest share of regional differences in the total fertility rate. Women in the Midwest and on the Frontier married at higher rates than those in the Northeast, and the higher incidence of marriage explained over 40 percent of the difference between the birthrates in those regions and the Northeast. The first two columns of table 1.4 illustrate the regional differences in the marriage rate and the ratio of men to women. But columns three through five of table 1.4 show that even after accounting for these differences, midwestern and frontier women had more children than northeastern women. Midwestern farm women gave birth to the largest number of children on average, and those who had probably completed their childbearing by 1860—those age forty and older, found in the fifth column in the table—had given birth to roughly 40 percent more children than their northeastern counterparts. The crude birthrate, the total fertility rate, and number of children ever born all show that farm women limited

11

Table 1.4 Proportion of Women Married, Sex Ratios, and the Number of Children
per Married Woman by Region, 1860

	Wives under 30 Years Old as % of Females 15–29	Number of Males per 100 Females 15 +	Number of Own Children Ever Born by Woman's Age		
			20–29	*30–39*	*40–49*
Northeast	34%	104	2.83	4.29	4.37
Midwest	42	110	3.13	5.34	5.81
Frontier	53	129	2.90	4.88	5.07
North	41	110	3.03	4.98	5.19

Source: Author's calculation from Fred Bateman and James D. Foust, *Agricultural and Demographic Records of 21,118 Rural Households Selected from the 1860 Manuscript Censuses*, magnetic tape, Indiana University, 1974.

their fertility in the most heavily settled regions of the Northeast compared to the less settled regions of the Old Northwest and beyond.

Although all of the studies cited identified a statistical relationship between differences in rural birthrates among geographical regions and the relative availability of agricultural land, exactly how land availability determined rural birthrates remained to be explained. The debate revolves around this question: Why in the middle of the nineteenth century did farm families in different regions of the North have different numbers of children? Or put another way, "Consider twin brothers aged 35 who had an equal start in life, are currently married, and are farm owners. The only difference between them is that one is a farmer in the East, and the other in the West. Why should the farmer in the East be more likely to show lower marital fertility than his brother in the West ?"[24]

Fertility rates fell elsewhere as well in the nineteenth century. Every European country except Ireland experienced the onset of long-run fertility decline by 1910.[25] This dramatic drop in birthrates continues to puzzle contemporary social scientists, and many theoretical explanations for this decline have been offered. Although these theories have been primarily designed to explain the general fall in Western fertility rates, they have also been employed to explain fertility differences between geographical regions at a point in time. Yet their performance when applied to the experience of nineteenth-century rural America leaves considerable room for further research.

According to one view, changes brought about by industrialization explain the long-run decline in Western fertility rates. The shift from household to factory production accompanied industrialization and weakened the patriarch's control over women and children in the household. Together these changes transformed the economic role of women and resulted in a decline in the economic role of children. One quotation, comparing the roles of women and children in agrarian economies with those in modern societies offers perhaps the best summary of the potential for change brought about by industrialization:

> The economic organization of relatively self-sufficient agrarian communities turns almost wholly upon the family, and the perpetuation of the family is the main guarantee of support and elemental security. When death rates are high the individual's life is relatively insecure and unimportant. The individual's status in life tends to be that to which he was born. There is, therefore, rather little striving for advancement. Education is brief, and children begin their economic contributions early in life. In such societies, moreover, there is scant opportunity for women to achieve either economic support or personal prestige outside the roles of wife and mother, and women's economic functions are organized in ways that are compatible with continuous childbearing. [26]

This passage paints a picture of fertility in pre-industrial and many contemporary developing regions, and shows how changes in the roles of women and children could eventually lead to lower birthrates. For women, an increase in opportunities outside the household meant an increase in the opportunity cost of motherhood; for children, a decrease in opportunities within the household meant an increase in their net costs. When the market value of a woman's time increased and that of children decreased, parents paid a premium in terms of foregone income for large families; thus, parents limited their fertility.

How well does this view of Western fertility decline explain the experience of farm families in the northern United States? Industrialization did change the economic and social roles of women and children. Children and young women could be advantageously employed outside the household in manufacturing during the early period of American industrialization. By the late nineteenth century, however, young women and children had largely been replaced in factories by men, often immigrants; women had begun working in the growing service sector at clerical occupations; and new technology decreased the demand for farm labor in general. In addition, mandatory school attendance and child labor laws passed in the latter half of the century prohibited a return to the large-scale use of children outside the house-

13

hold. Although these changes may help explain the continuing decline of birthrates in postbellum America, they do not explain the decline in rural birthrates that began shortly after the Revolution.

Furthermore, changes in the economic roles of women and children say nothing about the regional differences in fertility rates. The economic role of women and children might have differed as one went westward at any time during the nineteenth century. For example, women might have experienced more economic opportunities off the farm or fewer social constraints on market work in the Northeast than in the Midwest or on the Frontier. It is true that most manufacturing was carried out east of the Allegheny Mountains in 1860, and few opportunities existed outside the household for farm women in the recently settled Mississippi valley. But if married farm women in the Northeast had had more or better economic opportunities off the farm, then one would expect to find significantly more women working away from the farm in that region. In fact few farm wives maintained occupations away from the farm in any region. The two largest occupational categories among all farm women reporting occupations in 1860 showed 4.4 percent in domestic service and 0.7 percent as seamstresses.[27] These small percentages leave little room to explain the differences in regional birthrates shown in tables 1.1 through 1.4.

Of course the experiences of young women, particularly those who were single, and children of both sexes in northeastern manufacturing constitute an important part of U.S. labor history. But out-migration, to urban areas as well as to the frontier, plagued the Northeast from the end of the colonial period, long before manufacturing represented much of an alternative. The fact that a large proportion of young people in the Northeast migrated to areas of greater economic opportunity does not explain why those who remained had fewer children than those who migrated. Similarly, a greater proportion of the women in the Midwest and on the Frontier married than was the case in the Northeast, an observation consistent with the greater participation of young women in off-farm labor markets in general and manufacturing in particular in the Northeast. But even after controlling for the proportion of women who married, birthrates of midwestern and frontier families exceeded those of northeastern families by around 30 percent. Unquestionably, changes in the economy played an important role in changes in childbearing among rural populations, but there must have been more to the mechanism than industrialization and the resulting change in off-farm opportunities for women.

The role of children as producers ebbed in the second half of the nineteenth and early twentieth century. Consequently, children went from being investment goods to consumption goods; that is, the net cost of a child switched signs from negative to positive. The net cost of a child can be calculated in theory by taking the sum of the present value of expected outlays and the imputed value of parents' services, and subtracting the present value of expected returns from a child's output and the imputed value of their other services to their parents. It is possible that the net value of children switched from being positive to negative during the antebellum era, and that this shift induced parents to have fewer children. In other words, parents could receive a higher rate of return from investing their time and productive resources in other types of production or investment assets, investing in the "quality" of children as opposed to quantity, or investing in other forms of leisure than raising children—ideas that no doubt have crossed the mind of most parents at one time or another.

Studying the prices of slave children in the South offers one way to value children in agricultural production during the antebellum era. Early estimates of the net cost of male slaves showed that on average they were not net producers until after age eighteen. Assuming that the expenditures on free children before age eighteen exceeded those on slave children, then from an economic perspective free children could be treated as consumer durables, or net costs, as early as the middle of the nineteenth century. More recent estimates of the value of slaves, however, showed males yielded a positive net earning to owners at eight years of age and females even earlier, raising questions once again about the value of free children. Also, in many contemporary developing countries males become net producers at young ages, usually in their early or middle teens but often earlier.[28] The same could be said for northern children on antebellum farms. In the absence of explicit estimates of the value of free children, it is not possible to say at what age they became net producers; the fact that northern children were not assets, in the sense that they could not be sold, complicates such comparisons. Final judgment on this hypothesis awaits the explicit estimation of the value of the labor of free farm children in chapter 4.

A drop in infant mortality offers a potential cause besides industrialization for declining fertility. Declines in mortality can trigger birthrate declines. If families targeted the number of children they wanted, to obtain the desired family size when mortality fell couples would have needed to create fewer children—assuming, of course, that parents could control their fertility. Most European countries experienced declines in mortality before a fall in their birthrates. The American experience deviated from this pattern: mortality did not decline until relatively late in the nineteenth century, while fertility had been falling since the beginning of the century.[29] Thus it is difficult to make the case that changes in mortality played an important role in either the decrease of aggregate birthrates or regional differences in birthrates in the United States during the antebellum era. This conclusion assumes that families could control their fertility. If they could not, they would have found it difficult to control the number of conceptions, abstention being the only foolproof method. If a large proportion of the population did not possess contraceptive technology, or if contraception was not an acceptable alternative for a large proportion of the population due to religion or social custom, then the introduction of improved technology or its acceptance among previously noncontracepting groups would have led to declines in birth rates.

Two observations indicate that such a process of cultural diffusion of contraceptive technology played a significant role in the demographic transition in Europe. First, once marital fertility began to decline, in most countries it fell quite rapidly by historical standards. Within a few decades a revolutionary change came over this fundamental aspect of life, and a fertility regime basically uninterrupted since the Middle Ages collapsed. This observation suggests that a change in technique, and not some more subtle cultural change that might have taken generations before becoming widely acceptable, provided the impetus for the onset of fertility decline. Second, the spread of fertility decline seemed to follow sociolinguistic lines, crossing geographical regions, which suggests a diffusion of contraceptive technique along social or cultural lines. The importance of contraceptive technology hinges on the difference between desired and actual fertility. If relatively effective techniques of contraception are available and acceptable, then desired fertility will apparently equal actual fertility. Thus, the introduction of new contraceptive technology would have very quickly brought actual fertility down to the level of desired fertility. However, if contraceptive techniques were unavailable or unacceptable in a geographical area or among a particular segment of the population, this would lead actual fertility to exceed desired fertility.

Although inefficient by contemporary standards, contraceptive technology existed in antebellum America. Northern farm families had access to vaginal sponges and condoms from animal skins and organs as early as the 1830s, and rubber condoms became available later in the era. In addition, coitus interruptus was always an alternative, albeit an inefficient one, and by midcentury the rhythm method was well known. Until the nineteenth century fertility limitation resulted mainly from delayed marriage, but increasingly families limited childbearing within marriage, and the advance of contraceptive technology played a considerable role in the process.[30] If access to this knowledge or the acceptability of the practice differed by region in America, regional birthrates would have differed as well. Since cultural background helped determine the acceptability of contraceptive practice, farm families with different cultural backgrounds displayed different fertility patterns, as was the case in Europe. Following this logic, one explanation of East-West fertility differences could be that individuals from high fertility cultures (mainly immigrants) settled more heavily in the Midwest and Frontier.

In fact cultural variables, such as whether the household head was an immigrant, contribute in the statistical sense to explaining the level of fertility within a region. Furthermore, immigrant women on average gave birth to 17 percent more children than native-born women in rural areas of the Northeast: total fertility rates were 5.73 for foreign-born women and 4.90 for native-born women. In the Midwest and Frontier, the difference was even greater, with immigrant women giving birth to 22 percent more children than native-born women: total fertility rates were 8.23 and 6.73, respectively.[31] These figures show that immigrants in western regions maintained higher birthrates than immigrants in the Northeast, and the same is true for native-born women. While native-born women had on average 37 percent more children in the western regions than they did in the Northeast, immigrant women in the western regions had 43 percent more children on average than immigrants in the Northeast. So even after accounting for cultural effects on fertility rates, much of the difference in regional birthrates remains unexplained.

In their current form, the explanations of the secular decline of birthrates offered so far fail to explain more than a portion of either the temporal pattern or the regional differences in birthrates of farm families in the antebellum North. The key to explaining these differences lies in identifying how specific economic and social changes triggered fertility decline in the rural North. Economic explanations of fertility decline revolve, in one way or another, around changes in the direction of intergenerational wealth flows, such as changes in the economic roles of women and children, and a decrease in the value of children as producers.

17

According to one explanation of fertility decline, the rise of the "capitalist mode" of production, defined as the advent of production based on the selling of labor to individuals who are not members of the worker's household or family, changed the direction of intergenerational wealth flows.[32] Before modernization, wealth flowed from children to parents. The change in the direction of wealth flows arose because of increases in the amount of schooling children received, increased parental wealth, and the decline in religious influence, which extolled the virtues of hard-working and subservient children. As wealth flows changed direction, the capitalist system of production began offering goods produced in the market that substituted for home-produced goods. A relative price shift occurred that lowered the price of purchased commodities relative to goods and services produced in the household; thus, capitalism competed with the household mode of production, and women were simultaneously liberated and offered opportunities away from the home. Ideology represented an additional factor in this change, and the rise of egalitarianism—as indicated by, among other things, greater educational opportunities for young women—in turn contributed to the increasing opportunity cost of a woman's time in the home, leading to the further erosion of the older fertility regimes. This view of fertility decline emphasizes the effects of changing economic roles of women and children on the direction of intergenerational wealth flows, with the primary changes taking place through education, one of the most important means by which parents transfer wealth to children.

The antebellum era saw the provision of public education in many parts of the country, particularly in the Old Northwest. "Schools and the means of education shall forever be encouraged," stated the Northwest Ordinance of 1787. The great land ordinance equipped the settlers with the means of financing the rudiments of a system of public education by setting aside the proceeds from land sales in one section (one square mile) in each township for the establishment of a public school. But the establishment of complete public schools began only after a certain critical density of population had been reached. The Indiana constitution charged the state assembly, "as soon as circumstances will permit, to provide, by law for a general system of education, ascending in regular gradation from township schools to a state university wherein tuition shall be gratis, and equally open to all." Yet nearly fifty years after the passage of the Northwest Ordinance, George Forquer, an Illinois politician, wrote, "I must confess that, until our country becomes more densely populated, . . . I doubt the practicability of pre-

18

paring any coercive system of common schools which would be sustained by the people."[33]

If children spent significantly more time in school in the Northeast than they did in the Old Northwest, the cost in terms of both expenditures and lost opportunities in employment would have been greater in the Northeast, resulting in higher costs of children and lower birthrates in that region. Thus, differences in the level of primary and secondary education among the regions of the antebellum North could have determined the direction of net intergenerational wealth flows, with greater educational opportunities for children in the Northeast leading to lower fertility rates in that region. If this happened, one would expect school attendance rates to be significantly higher in the Northeast than in either of the other two regions. The evidence for educational attainment among antebellum farm children, however, points to more similarities than differences. Attendance rates in 1860 for farm children in households with both husband and wife living show that even in the most remote areas of the Frontier children attended school at relatively high rates: 70 percent in the newest areas for males ages ten through fourteen, and 68 percent for females of the same ages.[34] Children in the areas just behind the Frontier, in 1860 mainly the states of Illinois and Indiana, attended school at higher rates for both males and females ages ten through twenty than those in the older areas of the Northeast. In general, there was not much difference between enrollment rates in the antebellum Northeast and the Old Northwest.

The literacy or illiteracy of parents could not have played much of a role either, because even in the most remote regions of the Old Northwest the ability to read consistently reached above 90 percent for males and 80 percent for females.[35] Of course, regional differences may have existed between the amount and quality of instruction children received and the extent of parents' literacy that are not captured by the measures reported here, since both of these measures represent lower-bound estimates of educational attainment. For example, two individuals may both be literate, even if one left school shortly after achieving literacy while the other spent considerably more time in school.

A shorter school year and the labor demand for farm children in the Midwest might seem to indicate that midwestern children spent considerably less time in school than their eastern counterparts, but closer inspection reveals that this was not the case. A study of Ohio school districts, for example, showed that the six-month winter school year (October through March) in Ohio yielded on average about half the attendance days of the nine-month school year (September through May) in Rochester, New York, at the same time; however, Ohio children spent an additional twenty to fifty days in summer school, an opportunity not available to Rochester children, and summer school attendance made up for the shorter winter school year.[36] Although rural midwestern parents recognized an economic need for their children on the farm during spring planting and fall harvest, they desired an education for their children just as eastern parents did, so they sent their children to school during the relatively slack labor period in the summer. In other words, the regional differences in intergenerational transfers of wealth, as represented by the available measures of education, do not appear to have been large compared to differences in birthrates. Such a finding, however, does not rule out other means of intergenerational transfers as potentially important to birthrates.

The similarity in the long-run movement in aggregate birthrates of the United States and European countries gives the impression that the American experience might be explained by one of the theories of fertility decline reviewed earlier in this chapter. These theories explain how the diffusion of social, cultural, or economic conditions over different geographic regions led to fertility decline. Indeed, many of the most cited discussions of the demographic transition center on the process of the diffusion of fertility decline from countries or regions that have already experienced a demographic transition to developing countries that have yet to begin or are in the process of such a transition. During the post–World War II period, scholars employed various theories of fertility decline to explain the differences between nations of high and low fertility. Those same theories should be able to explain differences in fertility rates among geographical regions in the middle of the nineteenth century as well. Yet none of the theories convincingly explains differences in birthrates among rural areas of the antebellum northern United States, and the search for an explanation of these differences continues.

So far, we have rejected off-farm opportunities for women, contraception, ethnicity, and education as sufficient explanations of the pattern of rural fertility in the early nineteenth century, although these factors no doubt played some role in changes in household decisions, including fertility. Industrialization and education in particular can be viewed as parts of another explanation, namely, changes in the direction of intergenerational transfers in wealth and, thus, the net value of children. If the net present value of a child was positive in all regions of the North but greater in the Midwest or on the Frontier than in the Northeast, other things being equal, this difference might explain higher birthrates among farm couples in the newer regions. It could have been that by 1860 off-farm opportunities, agricultural practices, or other aspects of farming made the economic value of a child in the Midwest exceed that of a northeastern child. Or perhaps the net value of a child fell below zero in every region but had a smaller absolute value in the Midwest or on the Frontier than in the Northeast. In each of these cases, one finds the foundation of an economic explanation of the regional differences in antebellum birthrates. Children could have been either net assets or liabilities, but as long as differences existed in the value of children between regions, parents could have adjusted their fertility accordingly. Estimating the value of farm children represents a necessary step toward understanding childbearing patterns across the country during the nineteenth century.

Calculation of the value of a farm child involves estimating the relative costs and benefits of bearing and raising a child. In the absence of explicit estimates of the costs and benefits of children, however, it is possible to use available data on prices or wages as a proxy for the productivity of children. We saw that slave prices offered little help along these lines. Nineteenth-century wage data for hired male farmhands for different regions of the North show little regional difference, except for the Frontier where they were higher, but data on the wages of children in agriculture comparable to those available for adult males are rare.[37] If the wages of adult male farmhands accurately represented the opportunity cost of a child's labor, then fertility rates in the Midwest and the Northeast should have been similar, but fertility rates among those two regions differed markedly, as we have seen. Tables 1.1 through 1.4 showed that a gradient of birthrates extending roughly from the least to the most settled regions marked the antebellum North, with significant differences between the Northeast and the Midwest.

Furthermore, using the wage rates of adult male farmhands assumes that their wages represented the opportunity cost of child labor, but it is not clear that this was the case. If children took part in "farm making," which occurred primarily on frontier farms at the same time as farm operation, "the potential labor contribution of children was greater" in less settled areas in general due to a lack of "work possibilities" in areas of more settled agriculture. Thus, the opportunity to employ children in land clearing might have made them more valuable on the Frontier than in the more settled regions. In addition, the presence of fewer elderly individuals on western farms lent additional value to a child's help.[38] On the other hand, backbreaking work characterized the bringing of new land into production, while children probably realized their greatest value in the less physically demanding tasks associated with settled agriculture. Since the value of a farm woman's time was inextricably linked to the number of children she could bear and care for, the value of adult female labor must be estimated as well.

Costs are another component of the net value of children. The value of goods and services that children consumed represent one type of cost. For now, let us focus on another type of cost of raising children, which probably differed by region: bequests and inter vivos transfers (transfers made before the parent died). In this discussion, the term *bequests* includes inter vivos transfers as well. Eighteenth-century scholars and antebellum commentators recognized the relationship between land availability and birthrates, but neither they nor later generations of scholars offered an explicit theory of how the pressure of land scarcity manifested itself in the decline of fertility rates. The "targeted bequest" theory attempted to fill this void by explaining the regional differences in antebellum birthrates as a result of intergenerational transfers. This theory identifies four unique features of farming in the northern United States in the nineteenth century. First, farmers were generally well off, and they were interested in increasing their wealth and transferring it to the next generation. Second, farmers sought to provide their children with a decent start in adult life, and ideally this involved establishing them on a nearby farm. Third, mortality was low by the standards of American cities and of Europe, so that unchecked fertility would yield a large number of surviving heirs. Fourth, American farming was characterized by *multigeniture*—that is, the division of the father's estate equally among his heirs.[39]

Given these features of U.S. agriculture, the theory proceeds as follows. Assume that the farm couple's concern for establishing their children in adult life means that the parents desire to provide their children with a bequest of at least equal value to what the parents received when they were young and just starting their own household. If they themselves began adult life with $X worth of land, cash, or other property, it is assumed they desire to endow each of their N children with $X. Thus, a farm family needed to accumulate $NX amount of wealth before the children were ready to leave home, in order to meet this objective. Let us return to the question posed by Easterlin, Why would twin brothers living in different regions of the

North, but alike in all other aspects, have different numbers of children? The answer is now apparent. If their parents gave each of those brothers $X, then they in turn desire to give each of their children $X. The brother in the newer region will see his farm capital growing and appreciating in value as the region becomes more settled, but the brother in the older region will be pressed to keep the value of his farm from deteriorating. It follows that the farmer in the West can "afford" to have more children, in the sense that endowing them is part of the cost of raising children. According to the targeted bequest theory, differences in the costs of bequests explain the negative correlation between the extent of settlement and fertility rates found in many studies. Parents who make targeted bequests care about either the utility or satisfaction of their children, or about some unspecified social variable, such as the quality of their children's start in adult life. Parents display their concern by targeting some level of bequest; the theory specifies that in general the amount of the bequest equals or exceeds what the parents were bequeathed by their parents.

In a second category of bequests, called "strategic bequests," parents use the bequest as an incentive to get children to display certain types of behavior or supply a particular set of goods and services. For example, parents may promise the child a particular bequest, such as all or part of the family farm, if the child promises to take care of the parents in their old age.[40] Here altruism plays no role. Parents view children as a source of income while children remain in the household and as a source of financial security once they grow up and the parents reach old age. Children view their parents as providers of an endowment or bequest, the cost of which is the provision of farm labor while young and possibly old age care for parents later. A parent's use of the bequest as a bargaining tool to get children to behave in a specified manner constitutes the essence of the strategic bequest. "Land is the whip," as one farmer put it.[41] The intergenerational transfers between parents and children represent the outcome of a game played between the benefactors and their beneficiaries. Proponents of this view argue that in self-sufficient frontier areas families will grow until the marginal gain to parents' retirement wealth of an additional child equals the additional cost of raising that child. In a world with strategic bequests this result comes from "redundant" children undercutting each other's bargaining position, allowing parents to command a larger share of the wealth they have accumulated than they otherwise could. According to this view of fertility decline, parents' bargaining position eroded

23

when advanced stages of settlement brought more opportunities off the farm for their children; consequently, a decrease in birthrates followed.

Several historical changes contributed to the erosion of parents' bargaining power and the decline in rural birthrates. The passing of the Northwest Ordinance and the subsequent trans-Appalachian migration, the improvements in transportation that made midwestern agriculture profitable, and later the rise of manufacturing opportunities in northeastern cities all meant children could no longer be relied upon to remain nearby and take care of their elderly parents. Children might move to the Frontier to start farms of their own, or they might join the expanding working class in the growing New England industrial towns. These economic and social changes brought about the abandonment of agricultural areas of the Northeast and jeopardized the provision of old age security by children. The basic concept of *child default*—the loss of children as potential providers of old age security—lies at the heart of strategic explanations of the decline in birthrates.[42]

According to proponents of the strategic bequest theory, any explanation of the decline in farm family fertility must satisfy three criteria.[43] First, it must explain the onset and timing of the secular decline of rural fertility in the nineteenth century. The Malthusian "land scarcity" models fail to meet this first test, because fertility rates began to fall at exactly the time when land policies made endowing children with a farm easier than it had been in the past, even though the farm might be located several hundred miles from the original homestead. But why did the children need to be established on a nearby farm? If parents required geographical proximity for satisfaction or for the purpose of monitoring their children's welfare, the whole family could always move to the frontier. Second, a satisfactory theory must explain the cross-sectional differences in fertility at a given point in time. Numerous studies have shown that the land scarcity models pass this test fairly well. Third, either the land scarcity variables must be incorporated in a theoretical model of fertility decline, or a set of variables superior to them must be employed. The land scarcity variables explained rural birthrates, but they explained statewide birthrates including urban areas better than they explained rural birthrates, a result just the opposite of expectations. Thus, the correlation between land scarcity and rural fertility rates reported in so many studies may be spurious.

Note the contrast between the strategic bequest and targeted bequest theories. With strategic bequests, fertility rates decline as agricultural communities become more settled, not because the price of farmland rises, making targeted bequests more difficult to achieve, but rather because settlement brings greater opportunity off the farm, enhancing the bargaining strength of children. The strategic bequest theory presents parents as Machiavellian manipulators of their children's behavior. Parents play a game in which they use their wealth and ability to produce competing heirs as leverage to get their children to perform actions that the children otherwise would not perform. Targeted bequests, on the other hand, view parents or benefactors as benevolent dictators who derive satisfaction from their children's satisfaction by endowing children with real income and demanding nothing in return.

In spite of these differences, at least one important similarity exists between the two schools of thought. Supporters of both views claim that farm-making regions offered opportunities for the employment of children in the formation of farm capital that were unavailable in more settled regions. Settled agricultural communities, with an already high ratio of improved to unimproved acres, offered fewer opportunities of this type. Thus, a child's marginal contribution to farm capital in less settled regions was greater than in settled regions. This line of reasoning assumes either that the contribution of children to the production of crops and other agricultural output was smaller in more settled areas, or that the greater opportunity for the production of agricultural products in more settled areas was not enough to compensate for the contribution of children to capital production in less settled areas. By extension, this argument implies that farmers held what often appeared to contemporaries to be too much land, because an inventory of unimproved acreage could be employed to smooth the supply of family during slack periods. When the family was not busy planting and harvesting, children could be employed clearing unimproved acres. Again, children provided more wealth for their parents in areas with greater amounts of unimproved acreage, namely, the less settled areas. In more settled regions, the bargaining position of parents eroded as a result of the out-migration of children, rising nonagricultural wages and employment, and the rising rates of school attendance by children. "Parents could no longer rely upon their grown children to provide faithful labor on the family farm . . . Contributing to the reduced value of child labor on the farm was a reduction in their relative productivity."[44] In much the same way, the increase in animal husbandry, the practice of crop rotation, and the introduction of new crops in the East put an end to the farm's seasonal labor crisis. Children no longer provided a valuable service during labor crunches, and labor crunches were no longer an inevitable part of the economics of the family farm. Children became more valuable in agriculture the farther west one went.

All the studies discussed in this chapter addressing the value of antebellum northern children assert that children were less productive in settled agriculture. Yet the relative contribution of children to farm output in less settled regions has been debated. For instance, a strong argument can be made that children most likely made the greatest contribution in settled agriculture where they helped with gardening and dairying, tasks better suited to children's physical capabilities.[45] None of these studies directly estimates the contribution of women or children to farm output, nor do they estimate the cost of a bequest or the potential benefits from old age security, all components of the economic value of children. Once again the debate concerning the fall of antebellum birthrates revolves around the economic roles and value of children in agriculture; yet no explicit estimates of their value exist. Much of the rest of this book addresses this issue.

CHAPTER TWO

The Value of Output and the Division of Labor on the Family Farm

Travelers through the antebellum North often commented on the yields of the farms they found there compared to those of farms in their native lands, though they came to no consensus on the source of or reason for these differences. Some argued that natural fertility provided the bountiful harvests of the lands beyond the Appalachians. Indeed, despite what appeared by western European standards—and those of the growing group of agricultural reformers in the United States—to be decidedly primitive techniques, these lands generated considerable surpluses. Yields of 50 or more bushels per acre of corn were not unheard of in the Ohio valley shortly after settlement. "The Englishman began with laughing, or being shocked, at the slovenly methods of cultivation employed by American settlers . . . [yet] ended by following the American plan," declared Harriet Martineau.[1] "The fields are rudely tilled yet yield an abundant harvest," another traveler observed.[2] Others believed that the abundant yields were due to human labor. In general yeoman farms were inferior to those of the European estates, Alexis de Tocqueville maintained. "In America land is cheap, and any one may easily become a land-owner," he wrote, yet "its returns are small."[3] Despite this loss of efficiency, which he attributed to the small-scale nature of the freeholding system, Tocqueville reasoned that the industrious habits of American (democratic) labor provided surpluses in the aggregate nonetheless.

The progressive call of "scientific farming," as voiced by the agricultural societies and journals of the day, held a less sanguine view of the American farmer than did Tocqueville. "It would have been

27

difficult in any county to have found ten farmers who . . . had any system of farming or of agricultural economy," wrote an observer in one progressive journal.[4] Proponents of a more technologically advanced husbandry tirelessly complained that the land-intensive nature of American agricultural practice robbed the soil of its productivity. Critics cited the poor condition of livestock, lack of fertilization and crop rotation, and landholdings they considered to be too large to be farmed well by a single family as the primary deficiencies of the northern farmer.

A century and a half or so of scholarly research has produced the tools and knowledge, unavailable to contemporary commentators, to determine the source of U.S. agricultural success. Although soil type and quality vary greatly across much of the northern United States, in general the thick topsoil and the timing and quantity of rainfall in the Old Northwest provided an ideal environment for corn cultivation, and the prairie grasslands were well suited to corn and wheat. Other things being equal, the same agricultural practice—that is, the same quantity and quality of labor, fertilizer, and implements—would have brought forth higher yields of these crops there than elsewhere in the United States or much of Europe. But the institutional setting and the market conditions for inputs (land, labor, and capital) and outputs differed from region to region and across the Atlantic. American farmers, particularly those involved in the westward movement, wanted to farm as extensively as possible—that is, they used a great deal of land relative to other inputs. This mix of inputs in extensive farming differed from that of the new intensive husbandry employed by many western European farmers and advocated by progressive writers and farmers in America. The more advanced techniques of European agriculture increased the productivity of relatively scarce agricultural land. These techniques included considerable use of crop rotation, fertilizer, and selective breeding of livestock. The crop rotation patterns included fodder crops for livestock, which in turn provided manure for fertilizer and contributed to higher yields per unit of land.

In the United States the abundance and accessibility of land to a large proportion of the population made labor the relatively more scarce input. "In Europe the object is to make the most of their land, labour being abundant: here it is to make the most of our labour, land being abundant," Thomas Jefferson wrote in the eighteenth century.[5] Half a century later Harriet Martineau agreed; the English farmer in America "learns that he has got to a place where it answers to spend land to save labour; the reverse of his experience in England."[6] The relative scarcity of labor combined with abundant, fertile land meant that the output per U.S. agricultural worker surpassed that of all other western countries. On the other hand, intensive farming had been practiced in the low countries and parts of England for roughly two centuries before the Northwest Ordinance opened the western lands to U.S. farmers, and by the late antebellum era per acre yields in European grain farming, even in the backwaters of central and eastern Europe, compared favorably with those obtained in the Midwest.

American agriculture differed from that found in most of Europe in other respects as well. U.S. farmers were quicker to adopt the labor-saving innovations introduced in the 1840s and 1850s than were their European counterparts. The grain drill, mechanical reaper, and steam thresher all were brought into widespread use in the States. Only British farmers approached U.S. farmers when it came to the adoption of mechanical implements. Furthermore, data on output per worker indicate that even after accounting for differences in land and implement usage, American farm labor may have been more productive than European labor because of more "intensity of effort" among Americans, a claim Tocqueville probably would have agreed with.[7] Recent estimates of the productivity of agricultural land and labor for several European countries support the observations of contemporaries concerning the difference between the "European" and "American" ways of farming, though debate continues on the relative weights that should be assigned to the potential causes of these differences.

The average farm worker in the northern United States in 1850 produced 297 bushels of grain (corn, wheat, oats, barley, rye, and buckwheat) a year. The only country in which farm labor displayed a comparable level of productivity was Great Britain, which had an average of 223 bushels per worker. In general as one went eastward on the European continent the output per farm worker fell. French farm workers produced 98 bushels of grain a year, German workers 86, and Austrian workers 72. Estimates inclusive of livestock production tell the same story. By the late antebellum era U.S. farm laborers produced from 5 percent to 300 percent more output than their European counterparts. Depending on the country and the set of productivity estimates considered, and excluding Great Britain, no major agricultural producer in Europe had farm laborers even half as productive on average as those in America.[8] In contrast to the large differences in labor productivity, the yields per acre of crops grown in the northern United States and Europe differed little. While many European estates were better managed than yeoman farms, the inherent fertility of the land in the United States and its suitability for the production of these crops, especially in the Midwest, contributed to smaller differences in yields than output per worker. During the 1850s midwestern farms yielded from 12 to 17 bushels per acre of wheat and other small grains excluding corn. Farmers in the Netherlands typically obtained yields greater than 20 bushels per acre during the 1850s, and those in Austria-Hungary—hardly the most progressive country, agricultural or otherwise, in Europe—experienced yields in almost the same range as those in the Midwest, 11–17 bushels per acre, around the same time.[9]

The family-owned and -operated farm constituted the primary unit of production in antebellum northern agriculture. The organization and composition of the household; the location of the farm, including the climate, soil conditions, and proximity to markets; and farm size all played a role in determining the quantity and mix of farm output. In a quantitative study of the farm economy, however, it is important to know precisely what the term *farm output* represents. Economists employ the term *marginal productivity* when referring to the additional output obtained from adding more inputs, such as land, labor, and capital—that is, the change in total output or the value of total output with respect to a change in a particular input. For example, suppose a farmer hired an additional worker for a specific period of time. Given the current size of the farm, the number of family members, the value of implements and livestock, and so forth, how much would the output of the farm increase? The result would be the marginal productivity of hired labor. To estimate the marginal productivity of the various inputs one must have a well-defined measure of output. In the case of a farm that produced a single crop, such as corn, gross output would be the number of physical units produced, in this case the number of bushels of corn. However, none of the more than 10,000 farms in the Bateman-Foust sample limited their production to one crop. To avoid the problem of adding apples and oranges (or corn and wheat, to be more precise), I employ the total market value of farm output, or *gross farm revenue*, as the measure of output in subsequent analysis.

Conceptually, the estimation of gross farm revenue is relatively straightforward. The total value of crop output will be the sum of the product of the price and quantity of each commodity.[10] The eighth census (1860), source of the data employed below, provides either the physical quantity or the dollar value of 31 different types of farm products. The census recorded all of the crops by physical quantity, with the exception of orchard products and market garden products, which it reported by dollar value. In addition the census lists the dollar values of slaughtered livestock and any goods manufactured in the home.

Converting the physical quantities into dollar values requires prices for each commodity. The development of the interior transportation system during the decades preceding the Civil War facilitated the integration of regional output markets. In 1820 the prices of a collection of agricultural commodities in Cincinnati averaged only 57 percent of those in Philadelphia and New York. By 1860, the Cincinnati prices had risen to 84 percent of East Coast prices, but wide variances still existed in the regional prices of agricultural products. For this reason, local prices must be used, when available, to obtain the estimates of gross revenue. Table A.1, in appendix A, is a list of the products recorded in the 1860 census and the per unit prices northern farmers received for those goods. Although the collection of goods recorded in the census comprises a large number of products, most northern farms produced even more than those listed in the census. The census omitted at least four major sources of revenue, which must be estimated from other sources: poultry, eggs, fluid milk (milk not used in the production of butter or cheese), and lumber. Table A.1 includes the per unit prices of these commodities as well.

The sum of the values of the products listed in the census and those not listed yields the money income of the farm household, or the gross revenue of the farm operation in an accounting sense. For many purposes, however, this measure is not the "full income" of the farm household. The "new" economics of the household argues that families planned the allocation of their resources based on *all* the resources at their disposal, including their real wealth. The role that wealth transfers between generations play in fertility decisions justifies the use of this broader measure of income, which includes the sum of money income and returns to household wealth.[11] The returns to wealth, or unearned income as the Internal Revenue Service might refer to it, came from three sources: appreciation in the value of real wealth (farmland and buildings); appreciation in the value of livestock holdings; and the implicit rental value of the farm house—the value of the shelter services offered by the structures that otherwise would have been purchased by the family. Appreciation in the value of real wealth came from increases in the demand for land, a pure capital gain, and increases in the value of land from clearing unimproved acres,

31

a gain due to the labor that cleared it. Appreciation in the value of livestock holdings came from increases in the demand for livestock products and increases from reproduction.[12]

Not surprisingly, the importance of a particular crop or group of crops differed according to the region in which a farm was located. The extent of mechanization, which had a large effect on the allocation of farm labor, varied from farm to farm and between regions as well, and different members of the household often specialized in the production of certain crops or products. Thus, the economic roles and value of women and children may have differed according to the techniques of production employed and the extent to which they specialized in the production of particular products.

Field crops made up a large portion of the value of farm output. They included hay, corn, and other grains—primarily wheat, but also including, in descending order by total bushels produced, oats, buckwheat, rye, and barley. The production of these crops can be divided into preharvest, harvest, and post-harvest stages. Hay and cereals were the first crops for which production was mechanized to any great degree; by 1860 implements existed for the primary activities in each stage of production for most field crops, with the notable exception of corn.

The preharvest stage for cereal production required an initial preparation of the seed bed, often a two-step process involving tilling the soil with a plow, followed by harrowing. Plowing, a time-consuming and physically demanding task, was done either after harvest in the fall or the following spring. In the deciduous forests of the Old Northwest, trees had to be felled and the stumps cleared before extensive plowing could begin, though farmers often planted crops around the stumps during the first few seasons after settlement. On the thick topsoil of the prairie, small teams of men often specialized in breaking ground for new settlers at fees of $1.50–$5.00 an acre.[13] If the soil required further pulverization, as was generally the case, then harrowing followed.

Seeding, the next step in the preharvest stage, followed tilling or harrowing. Before the 1840s most American farmers sowed broadcast either by hand or with mechanical seeders that could be carried; seeders pulled behind a horse, however, became increasingly popular. The English farmer Jethro Tull developed a grain drill in the early eighteenth century, but it remained impractical until the last 1840s. Grain drills represented an improvement in seeding by measuring, planting, and then covering the seeds. Drilling led to a more efficient use of seed than broadcast sowing, so that less of the crop had to be "set aside" as seed for the next planting. In 1841 the Pennock brothers of Chester County, Pennsylvania, produced the first grain drill design to be employed on a large scale, and the years 1851 and 1857 saw major innovations in the grain drill, such as better metering of the seeds and covering of the seeds once planted. Although mechanization proceeded at a faster rate in the United States than in Europe, by 1860 farmers probably still sowed broadcast more than half of the winter wheat grown in the Mississippi valley.[14]

Until 1850, farmers planted corn with a hoe and followed the ancient hill cultivation technique employed by Native Americans long before the arrival of Europeans. During the 1850s hand planters replaced the hoe, and in 1853 George Brown of Tylersville, Ohio, patented the first successful mechanical corn planter. Many farmers "tarred" their corn before planting to inhibit birds from eating it, and this practice discouraged the mechanization of plating because the tar stuck to the planter. Another method of tarring used long after a practical planter had been developed consisted of pouring tar over the seeds before covering them with a hoe. Thus, mechanical corn planting remained less popular than the use of grain drills for sowing wheat until later in the century.

Although corn was in general a hardier, more pest- and disease-resistant crop than wheat, corn had to be cultivated, while wheat required little attention after planting. Farmers typically cultivated their corn two to four times before harvest. Until the 1830s, workers went through the rows almost exclusively with a how. After that time, however, farmers increasingly used horse-drawn shovel plows and cultivators to disrupt the weed growth between the corn rows, so that the plants required hoeing only around the stalk while they were still young.

Since antiquity the one-handed sickle had been used to harvest grain. To use a sickle, a person stooped to the ground, grabbed a handful of stalks with one hand, and cut them with the blade held in the other hand. The stalks were later raked, bundled, and shocked. The two-handed cradle scythe replaced the sickle in the late eighteenth century, and though it saved wear and tear on the back by eliminating the stooping that accompanied use of a sickle, a typical scythe weighed around 12 pounds and required strength and stamina on the part of workers. In May 1831 William Manning of Plainfield, New Jersey, patented a horse-drawn mower with a reciprocating sickle. Improving on Manning's idea, Obed Hussey successfully demonstrated his "reaper" to the Hamilton County, Ohio, agricultural commission in July 1833, and six months later he patented the machine. Perhaps the best known of these machines, Cyrus McCormick's reaper, became available in 1840. Europeans envied American farm machinery. According to one historian of technology, a McCormick reaper at the Crystal Palace Exhibition at London in 1851 "attracted more visitors than the famed Kohinoor diamond."[15] And little wonder: reapers increased the productivity of farm labor by roughly 50 percent. A team of eleven men could cut, bundle, and shock 11 acres a day with a scythe cradle, while a hand-rake reaper requiring an operator, a raker, and four bundlers could harvest 10–15 acres a day.[16]

Although operating a reaper lessened the physical demands of harvesting, until the self-raker became practical the operator had to rake grain as it was cut or someone else had to stand at the back of the machine and rake—and raking demanded stamina and coordination. Self-rakers first became available in the mid 1850s, and McCormick produced his first self-raker only in 1861. By 1860 as many as 150,000 reapers of all types may have been used by northern farmers, particularly on large farms.[17] Since arrangements existed for sharing and hiring out, farmers using reapers no doubt outnumbered the quantity of reapers available, but even at a rate of two farms to a reaper, fewer than a fourth of the 1.3 million northern farms in 1860 would have been using the machines. The number of farmers using reapers, however, understates the importance of the machines in terms of the proportion of the crop harvested, because larger farms found it more profitable than smaller ones to employ reapers. Although the majority of farmers still used relatively primitive techniques for the sowing of field crops and many farmers continued to use older technologies in harvesting as well, the adoption of mechanization on American farms surpassed that in all other countries.

When one considers these activities in the context of the division of labor among household members, mechanization becomes a paradox. On the one hand, except for plowing, which was among the most physically demanding of all farm activities, the primary premechanized activities, such as broadcast sowing and hoeing, involved a degree of physical exertion and stamina that even relatively young children could provide. The mechanization of these activities reduced the physical demands of labor employed in them even further. Moreoever, at least in the case of sowing wheat, the premechanized activity may have involved human capital skills that took much practice to acquire. Laura Ingalls Wilder wrote that a young boy "could not sow seed yet; he must practice a long time before he could spread the seeds evenly. That is hard to do."[18] In such a case the mechanized activity was less challenging. "Sowing by hand is after all an art, whereas most any woman or boy could drive a seeder or drill."[19] Adding capital to a fixed amount of other inputs would have increased output and also the productivity of labor and the value of children, leading to higher fertility rates. But mechanization also meant a family could farm the same amount of land with less labor, thus rendering some labor—for example, that of children—superfluous. So one cannot say unambiguously whether mechanization made children more or less valuable in the production of field crops.

In either case, observers noted that women and children did not typically perform field work in general or take part in the harvesting of grain in particular, which was arguably the most physically demanding task of antebellum farming after the initial clearing of the land and plowing. Harriet Martineau observed during her travels through the country in the 1830s that women generally did not perform heavy labor, such as clearing land and harvesting.[20] In Laura Ingalls Wilder's *Farmer Boy*, the tale of a year in the life of a farm family in western New York, only the threat of a late frost brought the mother and eldest daughter into the fields to help save the corn crop. They spent the rest of their time working in and around the house.[21]

After the cradle scythe replaced the sickle, the harvesting of hay and cereals became primarily the responsibility of the adult males, older boys, and hired hands on the antebellum farm. Women's labor increasingly turned to the household and barnyard, and they increased their production of dairy products in particular. The relative scarcity of hired labor the farther west one went, however, often meant that women and children had to pitch in at harvest, and one should not conclude that the division of labor was rigid. One Michigan farmer noted that "at this moment every man and boy, and even women are actively engaged in cradling, raking, binding, and shocking the golden harvest. I have seen hundreds of women near their log cabins assisting in the active duties of the field."[22] "The rule was, that whoever had the strength to work, took hold and helped," another farmer recalled. "If the family was mostly girls, they regularly helped their father in all the lighter farm work."[23]

Unlike the case of wheat, harvesting of corn did not become mechanized until the last decades of the nineteenth century. Corn did not require the timely attention at harvest that wheat did, wheat having a tendency to shed its grain if not reaped shortly after it ripens. During the antebellum era farmers harvested corn by cutting the stalks near the ground, binding the stalks in bundles, and then stacking the bundles in shocks. Later, often throughout the winter months, the shocks were unbound, the ears snapped, and the corn shelled. Farmers typically used hand-operated corn shellers, but in 1843 F. N. Smith of Kinderhook, New York, patented a horse-powered sheller. Cutting, binding, and shocking corn was demanding work, often done in poor weather during the late autumn. Since the demand for labor for the harvesting of corn was not as severe or concentrated as it was for the wheat harvest, the men typically could handle this responsibility unassisted. But snapping the ears and shelling either by hand or with a hand-operated sheller was a task that could be carried out by the whole family, and such activities occupied farm families during the long northern winters.

The postharvest stage of wheat production required first that the grain be separated from the head, a task called threshing. Like the shelling of corn, this work could be done during the winter. Before the introduction of mechanical threshers, farmers employed the flail—a long staff connected to a shorter one (the swiple) by a leather thong—to remove the grain. The threshing of wheat became partly mechanized when the Pitts brothers of Winthrop, Maine, patented their horse-powered thresher in 1837. After threshing, the grain had to be winnowed, or separated from the straw and chaff. During the early decades of the nineteenth century winnowers tossed the grain from a sheet or basket into the air so that the breeze would carry away the chaff, while the heavier grain fell back into the container. This was essentially the same technology employed by agricultural societies since time immemorial. By the 1840s, a hand-operated machine called the fanning mill separated the grain from the chaff and could be found on even relatively small northern farms.

Contemporaries noted that in a pinch women and children took to the fields, but they also claimed that in general a division of labor existed between field work, the domain of men, and other tasks nearer the household, which were the domain of women and children. The absence of women and children from the fields was not because they were physically incapable of performing many of the tasks; observer's who on occasion witnessed them in the fields attested to their ability to perform the required tasks. Instead, their general absence exemplified the division of labor within the farm household. A field hand during harvest consumed around 4,000 calories a day from three full meals and two "lunches" (one before and one after a midday dinner).

The farm wife and any children, particularly teenage daughters, or hired domestic help she may have had available often served the midday meals in the field. Since the preparation, delivery, and cleanup of these meals involved a considerable amount of time, it paid the family to have one group specialize in field work while another focused on domestic production. In this respect the family farm can be compared to a multidivision company. Such firms obtain the maximum output for a given quantity of an input by allocating that input among different activities until the marginal product equalizes across activities. Even though women and children may have been less productive in field work than adult males, occasionally, as at harvest, the value of their labor in the fields became greater than the next best alternative, particularly on farms with few or no teenage males or hired hands.

Domestic production, or work around the farmhouse, consisted of considerably more than running a catering service for field workers at harvest. As noted above, once the men gathered the harvest many chores remained for the whole family to carry out before the crop could be marketed or consumed. Furthermore, women performed or supervised the performance of a wide variety of year-round domestic chores, including cleaning, laundry, and ironing. Women followed a routine: "Wash on Monday, Iron on Tuesday, Mend on Wednesday, Churn on Thursday, Clean on Friday, Bake on Saturday, Rest on Sunday."[24] All the while they cared for children, of which there were most likely several. The average farm woman gave birth to more than five children and bore her last child during her mid to late thirties; thus, she was raising children well into middle age.[25]

Besides the everyday household activities, a wide variety of other tasks had to be performed, many of which fell to the woman of the house and the children and domestics under her supervision. These chores consisted of tending to the vegetables, dairy, livestock, and orchard products. Before the expansion of urban markets, the increase in average incomes, and an improved transportation network made large-scale production of fruits and vegetables profitable, women almost solely managed the care of the garden. In one family renting a small plot while saving for a farm of their own, the husband did several jobs while the "wife stayed at home raising garden produce which he hawked each day from a wheelbarrow to the townspeople."[26] Young women hired to help the farm wife with the domestic chores typically had no duties outside the household except tending the garden and milking. By the end of the antebellum period advocates of a more sophisticated agricultural practice suggested that farmers should respond to market conditions in the Northeast by shifting out of the production of cereals and into market-garden crops.

> We know of many farms not ten miles distant from New York [City], devoted to the raising of corn, oats, hay, wheat, rye, etc., in competition with western New York, Ohio, and elsewhere, and on lands, the interest on the value of which is as great as the fee simple of western farms. In our own neighborhood are many farmers who do not realize two percent upon the value of their farms while market gardeners in their midst are realizing comparative fortunes.[27]

On farms where market-garden, orchard, or dairy goods made up the primary products, the male head often took over the supervision of their production, though women and children, either from the family or as hired labor, generally continued to take part in the actual production.[28]

The responsibility for mowing and storing the hay and feed that sustained livestock during the winter fell to the men, but children almost always shared the responsibility of feeding livestock during fall and winter. Livestock often foraged for themselves much of the rest of the year, particularly in less settled areas. When slaughtering time arrived in the fall, everyone pitched in, though here again there seems to have been a clear division of labor. The men killed and butchered the stock, while the women processed it in the kitchen, and the children acted as carriers and helpers. "Father and Joe and John (two hired hands) dipped the carcass in the boiling water, and heaved it and laid it out on boards . . . All that afternoon the men were cutting up the meat, and [the boys] were hurrying to put it away . . . All the next week Mother and the girls were hard at work . . . in the kitchen" making sausage, headcheese, mincemeat, tallow candles, and lard.[29] "All that day and the next, Ma was trying out the lard in big iron pots on the cookstove."[30] The joint nature of these responsibilities makes it difficult to identify a clear division of labor in the production of livestock and related products.

Household manufactures represented such a large collection of items that identifying a division of labor for them collectively is impossible, but a significant portion of this category probably included yarn and clothing, and women clearly played the largest role in providing this source of income, though the responsibility of shearing the sheep fell to the men.[31] The census recorded many products in addition to these, and women and children helped with many of them. The two largest sources of noncrop revenue in the Northeast, wool and maple syrup, provided considerable opportunity for the employment of women and children. The children helped with cleaning the sheep before shearing and cleaning the wool afterwards, and the women processed the product from there. Children also helped empty the sap buckets during the production of maple syrup, and women processed the syrup into sugar once it was brought to the house. Although a clear division existed in the production of these goods, their processing, like that of livestock and home manufactures, displayed a jointness that makes it difficult to attribute their output to one type of labor or another.

Table 2.1 lists the dollar value per farm of four groups of products recorded in the census by region in 1860. Though northeastern farmers produced a greater value of field crops than those beyond the Appalachians, almost half of this figure came from hay production, much of which went to urban areas as fodder for horses. Excluding hay, farmers in the Midwest and on the Frontier produced corn and cereals worth 50 percent more on average than those in the Northeast. Better transportation facilities, access to urban markets, and competition from the Midwest in the production of grains led northeastern farmers to emphasize vegetables, market-garden and orchard products, and hay compared to the other regions. Climate, soil, and market conditions induced their midwestern counterparts to produce a greater value of field crops and slaughtered livestock. On average frontier farmers produced a smaller value of every category, although, excluding hay from the field crops, they produced a greater value of grains than those in the Northeast. Frontier farmers produced almost $100 in crops other than cereals and hay, in spite of the disadvantage of lack of access to urban markets. Much of this, however, came from the relatively large quantities of potatoes grown in the frontier regions of Michigan, Minnesota, and Wisconsin. Per capita potato production in those states was more than double that of the older midwestern states of Ohio, Indiana, and Illinois.[32] The large advantage northeastern farms show in the production of other agricultural products comes from a few specialized crops, such as maple sugar and wool, the production of which offered women and children important economic roles. Given the impressions left by contemporaries concerning the allocation of labor within the farm household, the results in table 2.1 show that the products that women and children specialized in played a larger role in the output mix of northeastern farms.

The crops reported in the census cover a large share of the average

Table 2.1 Average Dollar Value of Grains, Garden Crops, Livestock and Home
Manufactures, and Other Products per Farm by Region, 1860

	Grains & Hay	Vegetables, Orchard & Garden Crops	Livestock & Home Manufactures	Other Products
Northeast	$415.72	$233.14	$84.86	$48.84
Midwest	382.99	154.94	91.08	36.77
Frontier	265.87	93.10	59.20	15.51
North	409.41	159.89	85.05	35.17

Sources: Author's calculations from Fred Bateman and James D. Foust, *Agricultural and Demographic Records of 21,118 Rural Households Selected from the 1860 Manuscript Censuses*, magnetic tape, 1974; Lee A. Craig, "Farm Output, Productivity, and Fertility Decline in the Antebellum Northern United States," diss., Indiana University, 1989; and Craig, "The Value of Household Labor in Antebellum Northern Agriculture," *Journal of Economic History* 51 (March 1991): 67–82.

northern farm's output mix in 1860, but poultry, eggs, lumber, and fluid milk, which were not included in the census, also figured importantly in the organization of the farm operation and provided an important source of income for the farm household as well. Contemporaries claimed that dairy products in particular occupied a large amount of farm women and children's time. "It was the universal custom for women to tend the garden, just as they always milked the cows," recalled one midwesterner.[33] "Except in a Yankee family no man or boy could be induced to milk cows, it being regarded as woman's work," claimed another.[34] A third commentator noted that other than helping with the preparation of meals, hired girls had "no outside work except to milk the cows," though they frequently had to take care of the garden as well.[35]

While field work became increasingly mechanized, most dairying was done by manual labor. Women's absence from the field did not free them from heavy labor—far from it. One antebellum farm woman claimed, "I have made butter for twenty years, and worn out a good constitution churning and working and salting butter."[36] And when milk was particularly abundant, the men and boys had to pitch in and help, again showing how flexible the household division of labor could be. "The cows were giving so much milk that churning must be done twice a week. Mother and the girls were tired of churning, and on rainy days [the youngest boy] had to do it."[37] By 1860, churning remained the only aspect of dairy production that had been even partly mechanized. A sheep or a dog harnessed to a churn could convert into butter the cream of twenty cows a day.[38] Although churning in this way made up much of the production of butter in certain regions known for their dairy production, most northern farms still relied on the labor of a household member, usually a girl or woman. The average northern farm kept between three and five dairy cows, and the largest northeastern farms (those with more than 320 acres) averaged fewer than ten milk cows per farm.[39]

Subtracting the amount of milk needed to produce the butter and cheese recorded in the census from total fluid milk production yields the residual fluid milk. (Appendix A contains an explanation of the estimates of the physical quantity of total fluid milk produced in 1860.) Multiplying this figure by the price per pound from table A.1 yields the value of the residual fluid milk produced on each farm. Adding to this the value of butter and cheese production yields an estimate of the value of dairy products per farm. The first column of table 2.2 shows these estimates by region. Northeastern farms produced more than three times the value of dairy products of either midwestern or frontier farms.[40] Since the farmers in the Mississippi valley realized a comparative advantage in grain production, it is not surprising that those in the Northeast increasingly specialized instead in the production of goods for nearby urban markets. The production of fruits and vegetables discussed above illustrated this shift, and the same held true for dairy products.

The production of poultry and eggs represented another set of activities in which women and children provided a good deal of the labor: "The frugal housewife well knows the advantage of a basket of

Table 2.2 Average Dollar Value of Dairy Products, Poultry, Eggs, and Lumber Production per Farm by Region, 1860

	Dairy Products	Poultry	Eggs	Lumber
Northeast	$596.86	$10.06	$22.80	$43.39
Midwest	166.87	5.57	10.57	53.51
Frontier	160.60	3.81	6.03	6.71
North	472.97	7.08	14.72	39.73

Sources: Census Office, Eighth Census, Agriculture in the United States in 1860 (Washington, D.C.: Government Printing Office, 1864); Census Office, Tenth Census, Report Upon the Statistics of Agriculture Compiled from Returns Received at the Tenth Census (Washington, D.C.: Government Printing Office, 1883); Fred Bateman, "Improvement in American Dairy Farming, 1850–1910: A Quantitative Analysis," Journal of Economic History 28 (June 1968): 255–73; Craig, "Farm Output," chap. 3; and Craig, "Value of Household Labor," pp. 67–82.

eggs for the store . . . She has received many six-pences and shillings of 'pin-money' from the peripatetic chicken merchant."[41] When Laura Ingalls Wilder's mother-in-law left to visit relatives, she admonished her teenage daughter, "Be sure to gather the eggs every night . . . [and] to take care of the churning."[42] Appendix A explains the estimation of the value of poultry and egg production on northern farms in 1860, and the second and third columns of table 2.2 display the results. Together, the estimates of the value of these products show that on average northeastern farms produced more than twice as much as farms in the other regions—a not unexpected result, since poultry products were highly perishable and required a nearby urban market. Again, note that the goods that women and children specialized in producing provided the greatest income on northeastern farms.

Forests covered much of the Northeast and Midwest. Although an obstacle to the production of field crops, the forests provided important products for use on the farm and sale in the marketplace. Farmers in the deciduous forests of the Old Northwest constructed their homes, fences, and tools from lumber, and once settlement had expanded to the prairie, they exported lumber to that region. Stumps had to be burned out, and when market conditions and transportation facilities did not encourage the production of lumber, farmers often simply burned large quantities of felled trees as well. The ashes that resulted were refined into potash and, in a more purified form, pearlash and provided an input for such essential products as soap, bleach, dyes, and glass. The men felled the trees, and the women and children produced the refined products. "Mother was making softsoap, too. All the winter's ashes had been saved in a barrel; now water was poured over them, and lye was dripping out. . . . Mother measured the lye into a caldron . . . and the lye and fat made soap."[43] The fourth column of table 2.2 shows the average value of lumber per farm in 1860 by region. (Appendix A contains a description of the estimation of the value of lumber production.) As expected, the Midwest and Northeast dominated the production of lumber, with relatively little output on the frontier. The category of lumber does not capture all the value of forest products realized by a typical northern farm family. The category of home-manufactured goods in table 2.1 contains other lumber products, possibly including potash and pearlash, though these decreased in importance as time went by.

Adding the values reported in tables 2.1 and 2.2 yields one measure of gross revenue from the operation of the farm. But, the farm was more than a source of revenue: it also represented real wealth, the appreciation of which contributed to the full income of the farm household. In addition, it provided shelter for the family, hired labor, and livestock. Land constituted the primary form of real wealth in the rural North, and returns from landownership and the clearing of unimproved land figured in any calculus of the farm family. Numerous references exist concerning the ubiquitous habit of nineteenth-century Americans of speculating in the public lands. Contemporary sources generally condemned the absentee speculator. "Who would have thought that brokers, speculators and sharpers, could already have done so much to stigmatize the character of one of the finest domains that Nature ever offered to man," wrote one correspondent describing the Wisconsin Territory.[44] The word *speculation* used in this sense meant the acquisition of an asset with the primary intention of reaping a gain from an appreciation in its value without any tangible productive activity taking place. Yet individual farmers often speculated in land as well, although on a smaller scale than the land barons of the era. Observing this fact, an Englishman traveling in the antebellum North commented, "The people of the West became dealers of the land rather than its cultivators."[45]

The acquisition of land remained the foundation of northern agriculture throughout the period in question, and much of the discussions of farmers' wealth emphasized the returns from land, but a farm family's wealth also included the buildings, fencing, and roads that they constructed. The rate of appreciation in the value of the entire farm includes these assets as well as the land itself. In addition, farmers who owned their farms, including the house and structures, derived rents that they would have had to pay out had they not been owners.

Northeastern farmers derived almost twice as much in these implicit rents as did midwestern farmers and three times as much as did frontier farmers (table 2.3, first column). (Appendix A contains an explanation of the estimates reported in table 2.3.) Northeastern farmers invested relatively more heavily in their homes and other structures than did farmers elsewhere in the North. There are two major reasons for these regional differences. First, as we have seen, northeastern farmers specialized in dairying, indicating a potential need for more structures. The quality as well as the quantity of the structures on many northeastern farms, most notably those of the Germans in Pennsylvania, had been remarked upon for decades. Second, farmers in the Midwest often broke the land, built a sufficient dwelling, waited for the value of the farm to appreciate, and then moved farther west, so that they had little incentive to build elaborate structures.

43

Table 2.3 Average Increase in Dollar Value of Land from Improvements and Changes in Price per Farm by Region, 1860

	Implicit Rental Value of Structures	Gains from Clearing Land	Gains from Price Change	Total Gains from Land & Structures
Northeast	$97.69	$74.73	$246.24	$320.97
Midwest	51.35	122.11	160.56	282.67
Frontier	29.87	74.75	92.95	167.80
North	67.97	111.82	172.24	284.06

Sources: Census Office, Seventh Census, *Statistical View of the United States* (Washington, D.C.: A.O.P. Nicholson, 1854); Census Office, *Agriculture in the United States in 1860*; Jeremy Atack and Fred Bateman, *To Their Own Soil; Agriculture in the Antebellum North* (Ames: Iowa State University Press, 1987); Craig, "Farm Output," chap. 3; and Craig, "Value of Household Labor," pp. 67–82.

Between the Treaty of Paris and Gadsden's Purchase, the United States added 2.2 million square miles of territory. By 1860, 253 million acres of farmland in states other than the original thirteen had been added to the country's total—roughly 8.5 acres for every man, woman, and child, free or otherwise, in the United States at that time. Congress alone gave land warrants, which circulated as currency, for 64 million of those acres to soldiers of the previous wars and their dependents.[46] Much has been written concerning the disposal of the public lands, the relative merits of speculation, and who gained and who lost from wagering on the "national industry," but one finds surprisingly few empirical studies on the value or the sources of the gains or losses an average farmer might have realized.

Any historian familiar with the antebellum agricultural journals must be impressed by the number of commentators who believed that in general farmers overallocated their families' resources to land acquisition. Dozens of sources in agricultural journals from the 1830s to the 1850s lamented what they considered to have been the "overpurchase" of land. "No criticism of farmers during [the antebellum] period was more frequently reiterated than that farmers owned too much land," wrote one noted agricultural historian.[47] Some writers blamed the credit employed to aid pioneers in acquiring a tract of land, arguing that credit "encouraged men of small means to overbuy" land.[48] In the late 1850s many of the agricultural journals still offered critical opinions of the quantities of land farmers owned. For example, the *American Agriculturalist* in 1859 said, "If American farmers, instead of laboring to double the number of their acres, would endeavor to double their crops, they would find it a saving of time, toil, and an increase of profit. . ."[49] A year later in the same journal came this statement: "We have come to the conclusion that very few men comparatively are capable of cultivating one hundred acres of land perfectly; and we judge that by far the largest class would make more money if their acreage were positively limited to fifty, at most."[50] The *Ohio Cultivator* in 1858 stated that the old adage, "It should be the aim of every farmer to plant or sow one acre more," should be changed to "one acre less, with manure for the extra acre."[51]

Explanations of why farmers held this so-called excess land vary. Some commentators have argued that farmers held excess land for purely speculative purposes. "Practically all classes of frontier communities speculated in public lands."[52] Others, while agreeing that speculation represented one motive, have claimed that farmers held excess land with the intention of eventually improving it, "to be exploited at some future time," and that farmers purchased no "excess" land in any meaningful sense. Rather farmers held unimproved acreage as a device for smoothing labor supply during periods other than planting and harvesting.[53] In other words, maintaining an inventory of unimproved land provided a productive means of employing family labor during off-peak demand periods.

The role of unimproved land held by antebellum farmers has important implications for understanding the economics of the farm household in general and the value of women and children in particular. If farmers held land primarily for speculative purposes—that is, with little or no intention of its being improved by the present owner—then they may be viewed as speculators in the sense that contemporary critics used the term. Granted, individual farmers speculated on a small scale compared to the great speculators of the day, but if they mainly looked toward capital gains from an increase in the price of unimproved acreage, then one could view their excess holdings as "speculative." If, on the other hand, farmers held excess land in its unimproved state only temporarily, until it could be improved, then one might view farmers as mainly interested in the gains from improving land and as only residual speculators. This would be the conclusion drawn from the "labor smoothing" view of excess holdings. In actuality farmers probably followed strategies somewhere between these two extremes. But to what extent did they employ one strategy over another? And how large were the returns from either strategy, or some combination of the two?

The role of children in the amount of land owned and cleared must be addressed as well. Although men most often cleared the land, children offered what help they could, whether cutting trees or turning prairie soil for the first time. Harriet Martineau described how she encountered children futilely trying to help their father clear a farm site.

> One rainy October day, I saw a settler at work in the forest, on which he appeared to have just entered. His clearing looked, in comparison with the forest behind him, of about the size of a pincushion. He was standing, up to the knees in water, among the stubborn stumps, and charred stems of dead trees. He was notching logs with his axe, beside his small log-hut and stye . . . On looking back to catch a last view of the scene, I saw two little boys, about three and four years old, leading a horse home from the forest; one driving the animal from behind with an armful of bush, and the other reaching up on tiptoe to keep his hold of the halter; and both looking as if they would be drowned in the swamp.[54]

Both of the views of unimproved or "excess" land just described have two implications for the role of children in the farm economy. If the labor-smoothing view is correct, then farmers must have considered children valuable at clearing land as compared to other pursuits, such as gardening, dairying, or even going to school. And farmers intended either to transfer improved land to their children, to profit from farming the improved land, or to reap a gain from selling it in its improved state. On the other hand, if the speculative view is correct, then farmers found the allocation of their children's time more valuable in pursuits other than land clearing. Also, farmers intended either to transfer unimproved land to children or to sell it in its unimproved state.

It should be noted that some motives accounted for certain types of behavior with respect to landholding, which may not show up in subsequent analysis. Consider the case of a farmer who bought land during prosperous times with the intention of gradually improving it. A cyclical downturn might have induced the farmer to change his plans, perhaps even forcing him to sell the land in its unimproved state. This outcome would make the farmer's behavior appear speculative by the reasoning just described. On the other hand, consider the case of a farmer who bought land with the intention of selling it in its unimproved state. An increase in crop prices or an increase in the price of improved land might induce the farmer to improve the land rather than hold it in its unimproved state. This behavior would appear to confirm the labor-smoothing view of unimproved land; yet the farmer's original intentions were clearly speculative. A farmer might buy unimproved land contiguous to his farm rather than improved land elsewhere due to the costs of transporting labor and capital. In other words, historians observe only the outcomes and not the initial motivation of the farmers, but this information must suffice. "Clairvoyants and psychoanalysts may analyze 'intent' very well—judging whether buyers only intended to sell later at a profit. Most other scholars, however, can more usefully focus on outcomes."[55]

Despite the voluminous discussions on the gains from landownership, only a few studies offer quantitative evidence concerning the size of the gain an average farmer might have reaped from unimproved land, and these mainly focus on the returns from converting land from unimproved to improved status. From these earlier studies, we know that midwestern farmers realized a gain from improving 1 acre of $1.50–$5.00 by one set of estimates and $14–$25 by another set.[56] The higher range of estimates comes from the year 1850 and is based on the premise that "the average North Central farmer cleared 10 to 12 acres per new farm. The value of that work ran from say $140 to $200." Furthermore, amounts this high provided a "substantial incentive to buy and inventory land."[57] To gain an idea of the size of such a return to the average farmer, consider that the lower bound of this range would have roughly equaled a year's wages with board for a hired hand in the Midwest in 1850 and slightly less than a year's wages in 1860. Returns this high would have provided a valuable incentive for the employment of household labor in clearing land.

The comments of contemporaries suggest that the 10–12 acres cited as the average a north-central farmer would improve in a year is too large an area. An interesting series of debates took place within the pages of the *Ohio Cultivator* in 1859 concerning the best method for clearing unimproved land. Though the techniques do not concern us here, note that they all involved relatively heavy manual labor that pre-adolescent children could hardly have been very good at providing. More important, a few commentators noted the quantities of land they cleared. William Conklin of Erie County, Ohio, claimed that he improved 40 wooded acres in six years, while his neighbors averaged only 20–25 acres over the same period of time.[58] Lemuel Myers of Union County, Ohio, cleared 8 acres the first year he owned his 100-acre farm and 52 more acres over a twenty-year period.[59] Since these commentators were singing the praises of their own superior methods of land clearing, it seems that any bias in their estimates would be upward in nature. Yet these estimates range from 3 to 6 or 7 acres improved a year. Elsewhere, in the *New England Farmer* Thomas Haskell of Gloucester, Massachusetts, noted that he drained 7 acres in one year, and he claimed that this was no more or less than many of his neighbors had done.[60] Reports do exist of larger quantities of land being cleared in a year at this time. For example, the accounts of one farm, the location of which went unreported, appeared in the *American Agriculturalist* in 1858: the farmer cleared 15 acres with a return of $15 an acre. The editors noted, however, that $15 per acre seemed reasonable only for a farm located "near a good market," and not for an average farm. In addition, the value of this farm was $3,600, which placed it considerably above the mean in 1858, a year following one of the century's worst recessions. Clearly, this was an exceptional farm.[61]

Another way of estimating how much land the average farmer might have cleared per year between 1850 and 1860 is to use aggregate data. In the frontier and midwestern states, 26.5 million more improved acres existed in 1860 than in 1850, along with 70 percent more farms, an increase from 437,000 to 741,000. If farmers already farming in 1850 cleared as much as 50 percent of the land cleared between 1850 and 1860, then they would have averaged only 3 acres a year newly cleared. If all the land had been cleared by the 437,000 farmers who were farming in 1850, they would have averaged only 6 acres a year. Even if all the land had been cleared by the 304,000 new farmers between 1850 and 1860, they would have averaged fewer than 9 acres a year.[62] Thus, both narrative and quantitative evidence points to 5 or 6 acres as the amount an average farmer cleared a year.

In addition, the average increase in the value of an acre from improving it probably fell below the $14–$25 range cited. In equilibrium the value of improving an acre of land should equal the market price of the labor and capital services that go into improving it. In other words, the difference between the value of an improved acre and an unimproved acre should have equaled the cost of improving it; otherwise, unappropriated rents would have existed, and farmers could have profited from employing capital and labor to clear more land. A survey of the costs of breaking land in the Midwest between 1850 and 1860 from more than twenty sources shows that in no case did the cost exceed $13 an acre, with a median value of $2.19 an acre.[63] Improving land often involved other activities, such as fencing, but these costs averaged only a few additional dollars per acre.[64] Thus, the $140–$200 reported as the average gain an antebellum midwestern farmer might have received from clearing land probably exceeds the actual amount.

The second and third columns of table 2.3 display the results from estimating the gains from clearing land and from an increase in the price of land. (Appendix A contains an explanation of the derivation of these gains.) Notice that in every region the gains from changes in prices—a reflection of increases in the demand for land or the speculative motive—dominated the gains from improving land. The greatest difference existed in the Northeast. By 1860 a larger proportion of all the farmland ever cleared in the Northeast had already been cleared than was the case in either of the other two regions, so it makes sense that the gains from clearing land should be smaller in that region. Conversely, the less market-oriented nature of agriculture and relatively large supply of land on the Frontier meant lower prices and less land cleared in that region.

Perhaps surprisingly, the increases in farm values due to increases in the demand for land dominated those from clearing land in the Midwest as well, no doubt a reflection of the increased value of land as a result of improvements in the transportation system during the 1850s. In every region farmers derived a significant share of the total return from land from clearing and improving as well as from pure capital gains. Farmers purchased more land than they could have reasonably expected to farm in the near future with plans to employ family labor in clearing and to endow children in the future, and the prospect of internal improvements and increasing market accessibility led to the hope of a capital gain. Thus farmers pursued a strategy somewhere between "peasant and gambler."[65]

The final column in table 2.3 shows the sum of the first three. The large gains from increases in the demand for farm land and implicit rents that accrued to farms near the urban areas of the Northeast show up clearly. The total returns from land and structures in the Northeast exceeded those of the other regions, and the returns decreased as one went westward. Overall, the average northern farm family realized around $280 a year from increases in the value of the farm, but only about $110 of that came from clearing land, considerably below the $140–$200 range cited earlier. Furthermore, the nineteenth century saw numerous "boom and bust" cycles in land sales. Eighteen fifty, the year from which the $140–$200 range of estimates came, was near the trough of one such cycle; therefore, the returns from that year represent the lower end of the spectrum of potential gains in this era. Comparing the estimates from 1850 with the average gains from land clearing throughout the 1850s clearly shows that the figures for 1850 are too high. Even the region with the largest average gains from clearing land displayed a value of $122, below the lower bound of $140 for the 1850 estimate.[66]

Although not insignificant, the gains from improving land in general fell well short of the combined value from dairy, market-garden, and poultry products. Women and children dominated the production of all of these other products according to the accounts of contemporaries, and all of these goods contributed greater value to farm output in the Northeast than elsewhere. The results in tables 2.1–2.3 lead one to be suspicious of the assertions of economic historians and demographers cited in chapter 1 who have claimed that children must have been more valuable in clearing land on the frontier than in other pursuits. The evidence so far indicates that the activities that children seemed well suited for, and that contemporaries claimed women and children participated in the most, yielded the greatest income not in the least settled regions of the North but rather in the Northeast, the most heavily settled region.

The sum of income from farm operations and returns from wealth yields a gross revenue figure for the farm as a firm, or the full income of the farm household. Since tenants did not realize increases in the value of the land they farmed, these figures varied by the type of tenure as well as by region. A farm that had a value less than or equal to the value of real estate held by the head of the household defines an *owner-operator farm*. The definition of a *part-owner farm* is one on which the value of real estate was less than the value of the farm but greater than zero. If the head of the household owned no real estate, then that was a *tenant farm*. Many travelers through the rural North during the antebellum era claimed that farm ownership was nearly universal. For each region, table 2.4 shows the percentage of farms of a particular type of ownership, in parentheses under the estimates of gross revenue. These percentages support the claims of those antebellum observers. In no region did more than 12 percent of the farm families own no land, and in every region more than 80 percent owned all the land they farmed. At least this aspect of Jefferson's vision survived the onset of industrialization.

Table 2.4 also presents the results of the estimation and aggregation of the different components of farm revenue reported in the previous tables. The table lists average full income for the farms in each ownership category and region of the North. The results show that yeoman farms yielded higher gross revenues than tenant farms, and the differences were greater in the Midwest and on the Frontier than in the Northeast. Part-owners had the highest levels of gross revenue among

Table 2.4 Average Gross Revenue per Farm by Region and Type
of Ownership, 1860

	Owner-Operator (% of total)	Part-Owner (% of total)	Tenant (% of total)	Regional Mean (% of total)
Northeast	$1,635.51	$1,725.93	$1,457.37	$1,627.84
	(86.92)	(5.82)	(7.26)	(100.00)
Midwest	947.36	1,021.53	674.14	921.74
	(82.51)	(6.38)	(11.11)	(100.00)
Frontier	783.25	937.49	637.56	777.63
	(81.39)	(7.17)	(11.45)	(100.00)
North	1,168.77	1,231.00	867.71	1,143.11
	(83.86)	(6.31)	(9.83)	(100.00)

Sources: See tables 2.1–2.3.

Note: Figures in parentheses are the percentage of farms in the region characterized by that type of ownership. Components do not sum to total because capital gains accrue to owner-operated farms only.

the three ownership groups. A significant proportion of these differences reflects differences in the size of the holdings of land of the various groups. Larger farms experienced both greater quantities of output and higher returns to wealth, and in general part-owners had larger farms than yeomen, while yeoman farms were larger than tenant farms. The average sizes for farms in the Midwest are shown in table 2.5.

The per capita farm income of the entire North, after accounting for wages, depreciation, and rents, was $155, though per capita income in the Northeast was more than 50 percent higher than in the other regions. These figures approximate those for per capita national income of the free population for the entire country, and the regional distributions coincide with those reported elsewhere as well.[67] Thus, my estimates of farm income for 1860 indicate that northeastern farm dwellers experienced a standard of living considerably above the national average. Farm families living in the Midwest experienced a standard of living close to the national average, and those on the Frontier probably experienced a standard of living below the national average. Overall, midwestern and frontier dwellers however, were relatively prosperous, since in current (1992) dollars they had per capita incomes greater than most of the world's population today.

Numerous contemporary accounts of the division of labor within the farm household indicated that women and children typically worked in the dairy, the garden, and around the house. Men and teen-

51

Table 2.5 Average Sizes of Farms in Midwest, by Type of Ownership, 1860

	Improved Acres	Unimproved Acres	Ratio
Part-owner	88	69	1.28
Owner-operator	68	61	1.11
Tenant	53	47	1.13

age boys, on the other hand, were more likely to work in the fields. The products that came from the "women's work" made up a larger share of the value of output on northeastern farms, and these farms were on average more prosperous than those farther to the west. These findings lead one to suspect that, excluding the costs of bequests and the benefits of old age security, children were more valuable in the low fertility Northeast—an anomalous result considering the literature discussed in chapter 1. At the same time, other commentators noted that when pressed by the weather or market conditions, most household members performed whatever tasks they could whenever those tasks needed to be done, thus mitigating the significance of any division of labor within the household. Before turning to the estimates of the value of children, it would help our understanding of the economics of the family farm to know if the production of a particular mix of output was determined by the composition of the household.

CHAPTER THREE

The Allocation of Farm Labor and the Life Cycle of the Household

The descriptions left by contemporary commentators, discussed in chapter 2, show that women and children played important and often specific roles in antebellum northern agriculture. Observers remarked that women and children specialized in producing particular products, especially dairy, poultry, and truck-farm products. Yet travelers could comment reliably only on what they actually saw in those areas that they actually visited, and most farm women and children at one time or another probably performed all the tasks that men usually performed. Indeed, narrative evidence exists in support of such a claim. Differences in the importance of the products women and children supposedly specialized in might be expected to correlate with regional differences in rural birthrates. Paradoxically, the products that contemporaries attributed to children proved to be more important sources of income on northeastern farms than elsewhere, but northeastern farm families had the lowest birthrates in the antebellum North. This observation does not prove that farms with children produced significantly larger quantities of these products than farms without children. In other words, the key question is, Did farms with children derive a greater proportion of their revenue from the activities children supposedly specialized in than did farms without children, regardless of the region in which a farm was located?

The answer to this question requires information beyond the regional means of the value of output reported in chapter 2. Narrative evidence, though infrequent, subject to bias, and often contradictory, nonetheless yields hypotheses from which to construct an economic explanation of regional fertility. For example, one hypothesis is that women and children specialized in the production of particular crops, regardless of region. It follows that regions with high birthrates should have produced larger amounts of crops in which children specialized, but the results presented in chapter 2 showed just the opposite. Northeastern farms specialized in dairy and truck-farm products, and midwestern and frontier farms in field crops and farm making.

The question of whether farms with children actually produced "women's and children's" products can be tested by first dividing farm revenue into several categories, according to the type of household labor most likely to be involved in the production of items in each category. After dividing output into categories, the farms must be divided according to the composition of their households. Certainly, regional differences in the mean value of output presented in chapter 2 provide an interesting picture of the rural economy, but such evidence may well have misled earlier scholars. By trying to ascribe regional fertility differences to differences in the economic activities of children, they overemphasized the role of children in land clearing. The narrative evidence indicates that differences in output mix existed among different types of households within as well as among regions. Did northeastern farms with no children derive as much income from dairy products as those with teenagers or young children? Did farms in the Northeast with no children produce a different mix of outputs than those in the Midwest with no children? Did farm size make a difference? The answers to these questions require the categorization of households based on the life cycle of the farm family.

Throughout the literature of the social sciences one finds issues pertaining to changes in consumption and the allocation of resources over an individual's life cycle. Much empirical evidence on life cycle behavior comes from cross-sectional data, such as those used in this study, in which the age of the head of the household is employed to determine the life cycle stage of the household or family as well. Such an approach may present problems when using cross-sectional data. For example, dividing households by the age of the head creates the dilemma of trying to explain dynamic behavior—that is, behavior that takes place over time—with static data. Research on the proportion of extended or "stem" households in eighteenth-century Austria identified this problem, showing that what appeared cross-sectionally to be two different types of households turned out to be households of the same type but at different developmental stages.[1]

A related problem applies to questions concerning the economic roles of children. It is possible that two households with heads of very different ages might might have the same structure with respect to other members of the household. For example, a twenty-year-old head of a household and a forty-year-old head of another household are at different stages in their personal life cycles, but the composition of their households could be identical. The twenty-year-old could have two young children and a forty-year-old aunt and uncle living with him, or a forty-year-old hired hand and his wife, while the forty-year-old head could have a twenty-year-old son and his wife and two young children living in the same household. In either case the potential pool of household labor remains the same.

To avoid the problem of mistaking two households of the same type or developmental stage as different because the heads have different ages, I define new stages of household structure that rely on the ages of children as well as the age of the head. Stage I of the family, as opposed to the individual, life cycle occurs when a husband and wife leave the households of their parents but have not yet had children of their own. Stage II is when the household contains only young children, less than thirteen years old. The family reaches stage III when the household contains both young children and teenagers younger than eighteen. Stage IV occurs when the household contains only teenage children. Stage V is when a household contains no children but has an older head, defined here to be someone over forty. Since the median age of marriage in the antebellum North was between twenty and twenty-five, the vast majority of heads who were ever going to be parents would have begun having children by forty.

Until they reached their teens, boys and girls on northern farms performed many of the same chores. Upon reaching their teens, however, the young men typically performed different tasks than the young women, and the differences in responsibilities continued through adulthood. To account for these differences in the work of teenage boys and girls, the stages of the household life cycle that include teenagers (stages III and IV) are defined for boys only. The reason for this lies in the change in the type of work children did once they reached puberty. Boys went to the fields; girls, while occasionally reported to have labored in the fields during periods of peak demand, such as harvest, mainly stayed around the house, working in the home, garden, and dairy. This classification made little difference in the statistical results reported here, but it does provide a better test of the hypothesis that different types of households operated different types of farms than would have been possible by combining teenagers of both sexes.

55

The family nature of the organization of northern agriculture prohibits further categorization with respect to adult females. Farms without at least one grown woman and one grown man made up less than 2 percent of the sample; thus, it is difficult to compare the output mix of farms with only one or the other to farms with both.

The farm was more than just the home of a family of farmers: it also represented a firm, and the farmer had considerable leeway in determining the composition of the farm work force. Labor could either be produced in the form of children or hired in the spot market as hired hands and their families. This freedom justifies the categorization of households by the life cycle stage of the family rather than by that of the head of the household. Once the household has been identified by life cycle stage, the question becomes whether or not the presence of children correlated with the production of certain types of output. To test this hypothesis, we first divide the farms by both region and the composition of the household. Recall that each farm in the sample comes from a specific geographic region—Northeast, Midwest, or Frontier—and that within the regions each farm can be identified with one of the five life cycle stages just described. Second, we test to see whether households in different regions but at the same stage in the family life cycle had the same output mix. That is, did they derive the same proportion of household income from the same types of output? Third, we test to see whether households within the same region but at different stages in the family life cycle had the same output mix.

Not surprisingly, households with both young children and teenage boys (stage III) constituted the largest ones in each region (table 3.1). Among those who owned all or part of the land they farmed, stage III families also owned the largest farms (table 3.2). In each region, households grew during the first three stages, then shrank toward the end. Although part of this pattern can be attributed to how the stages are defined, the pattern is consistent with life cycle theory in two respects. First, since other members of the household represented human capital, and since human capital generated wealth, we would expect that the pattern of initial accumulation and subsequent divestment generally found for other forms of wealth would be followed by human capital. Second, the pattern of initial wealth accumulation followed by a decrease fits the pattern of increasing then decreasing household size, which supports the theories of bequests discussed in chapter 1. As families aged they accumulated assets with income generated partly by the human capital embodied in children. Eventually, the process of accumulation ended, and intergenerational transfers changed di-

56

Table 3.1 Life Cycle Stage and Household Composition: Number of Persons per Farm in Each Age/Gender Group by Region, 1860

Life Cycle Stage	Children & Teenage Females		Teenage Males		Adult Females		Adult Males		Total	
	Owners	Tenants	Owners	Tenants	Owners	Tenants	Owners	Tenants	Owners	Tenants
Northeast										
I	—	—	—	—	1.27	1.22	1.31	1.32	2.58	2.54
II	2.53	2.87	—	—	1.42	1.26	1.57	1.31	5.52	5.44
III	2.73	3.15	1.27	1.33	1.53	1.39	1.64	1.53	7.17	7.40
IV	—	—	1.16	1.22	1.63	1.57	1.61	1.64	4.40	4.43
V	—	—	—	—	1.51	1.55	1.66	2.00	3.17	3.55
All Farms	1.93	1.87	0.42	0.26	1.46	1.34	1.58	1.44	5.39	4.91
Midwest										
I	—	—	—	—	1.03	1.11	1.22	1.21	2.25	2.32
II	3.09	2.86	—	—	1.20	1.07	1.41	1.14	5.70	5.07
III	3.44	3.41	1.37	1.28	1.37	1.14	1.61	1.33	7.79	7.16
IV	—	—	1.29	1.29	1.54	1.43	1.66	1.50	4.49	4.22
V	—	—	—	—	1.31	1.31	1.61	1.92	2.92	3.23
All Farms	2.75	1.88	0.53	0.28	1.27	1.17	1.49	1.38	6.04	4.71
Frontier										
I	—	—	—	—	0.92	1.06	1.28	1.22	2.20	2.28
II	2.94	3.16	—	—	1.11	1.12	1.48	1.47	5.53	5.75
III	3.36	3.47	1.34	1.25	1.26	1.19	1.59	1.66	7.55	7.57
IV	—	N.O.	1.21	N.O.	1.18	N.O.	1.59	N.O.	3.98	N.O.
V	—	N.O.	—	N.O.	1.27	N.O.	1.93	N.O.	3.20	N.O.
All Farms	2.58	1.81	0.44	0.26	1.14	1.11	1.50	1.45	5.66	4.63

Source: Author's calculation from Fred Bateman and James D. Foust, *Agricultural and Demographic Records of 21,118 Households Selected from the 1860 Manuscript Censuses,* magnetic tape, Indiana University, 1974.

Note: "Owners" includes part-owners. N.O. ("no observations") means there were fewer than 10 farms in that category.

Table 3.2 Life Cycle Stage, Gross Revenue, and Real Wealth per Farm by Region, 1860

Life Cycle Stage	Gross Revenue		Value of Real Estate		Value of Capital Stock		Value of Livestock		Total Number of Acres	
	Owners	Tenants	Owners	Tenants	Owners	Tenants	Owners	Tenants	Owners	Tenants
Northeast										
I	$1,220	$1,063	$2,875	—	$103	$100	$379	$385	102	102
II	1,494	1,164	3,458	—	119	113	461	405	112	122
III	1,930	1,224	4,747	—	158	133	623	478	136	113
IV	1,715	2,623	3,975	—	131	145	538	681	118	133
V	1,416	781	3,622	—	117	45	436	263	103	85
All Farms	1,641	1,457	3,807	—	129	112	500	417	117	113
Midwest										
I	$ 815	$822	2,017	—	$ 69	$65	$316	$319	103	114
II	1,014	584	2,552	—	88	57	388	257	116	82
III	1,351	826	3,699	—	123	69	536	333	158	134
IV	1,165	709	3,472	—	104	62	443	366	138	108
V	1,057	613	3,025	—	96	40	412	253	123	184
All Farms	952	674	2,975	—	100	62	438	295	131	104
Frontier										
I	$707	$810	$1,837	—	$51	$ 80	$232	$395	160	147
II	856	714	1,799	—	69	78	304	284	140	118
III	1,077	702	2,453	—	92	105	383	319	161	131
IV	775	N.O.	1,591	N.O.	77	N.O.	351	N.O.	125	N.O.
V	896	N.O.	1,702	N.O.	62	N.O.	350	N.O.	101	N.O.
All Farms	795	750	1,987	—	74	85	322	329	137	130

Source: Author's calculation from Bateman and Foust, *Agricultural and Demographic Records*, tape.
Note: "Owners" includes part-owners. N.O. ("no observations") means there were fewer than 10 farms in that category.

rection. On owner-operated farms gross revenue, the value of real estate, the value of implements and livestock, and farm size increased during the early stages of the family life cycle and declined toward the end.

The pattern of wealth over the life cycle coincides with the observation that some farmers transferred land to children either through outright gift (altruism), sale, or some other form of (strategic?) exchange. The presence of an increasing tendency to deed land to children rather than willing it to them after death, which had been present as early as the colonial period, may have resulted from a decline of the relative bargaining power of parents.[2]

As opportunities for children away from the family farm increased, the promise of land may not have been enough to keep them on the farm, so that parents found it necessary to turn over a portion of their land to their children before their own death. This pattern follows the predictions of the strategic bequest hypothesis. Although on average antebellum parents died only a year or two after their last child married, risk-averse parents would have tended to purchase insurance to avoid the loss of some proportion of future income due to financial disaster or physical incapacity, and giving children land with the stipulation that the parents be provided for represented one form of old age insurance.[3]

Northeastern farmers on average maintained a greater value of real estate than did those in the other two regions, and as a group northern farmers typically possessed real estate of greater value than the national average for real wealth. All of the owner-operator groups shown in table 3.2 owned mean wealth greater than the national average of $1,492 in 1860.[4] The greater value of northeastern farms shows up in real estate, implements, and livestock, but not in overall farm size. On average, total farm size increased as one moved westward, and the average number of total acres varied from a low of 104 for midwestern tenants to a high of 137 for owners on the Frontier. The mix between improved and unimproved acres differed considerably among regions. More than two-thirds of all land on northeastern farms consisted of improved acres, while the proportion fell to just over one-half in the Midwest and one-third on the Frontier. These figures point out the importance of owning a farm for a period of time and having an urban market nearby. The history of American agriculture evokes pictures of the frontier family felling trees or plowing virgin prairies and subsequently cultivating seemingly endless acres of corn and wheat. However true such visions may have been for a particular type of family, they omit the important role of the established northeastern dairy and truck farmer who supplied cities and nonfarm workers of the region with fresh produce, poultry, and butter and cheese. Location made these farms more capital- and livestock-intensive and generally more committed to scientific farming than farms in either of the other two regions.

In his treatise *The Theory of the Peasant Economy*, the early twentieth-century Russian economist A. V. Chayanov recognized the significance of the size and composition of the household to the economy of the family farm. Chayanov argued that the peasant farmer should choose a crop portfolio "which will give the highest and most stable payment for [family] labor," and should "determine the desired size of field cultivation applicable to [the] farm family."[5] Further, he argued that the composition of the household plus any additional labor that might be hired during harvest determined the extent of the farm operation.[6] Elsewhere, however, he recognized that location played an important role as well, noting that "climatic conditions [and] . . . the location of the farm in relation to the market . . . ha[ve] no less, if not greater, significance."[7] Thus, climate, soil conditions, and proximity to markets signaled farmers to produce certain products, while the type of family labor available may have signaled the production of other products.

Chayanov did not work through the logical implications of his arguments concerning the relative importance of these potentially conflicting determinants of crop mix and farm size. Yet identifying the relative strengths of these two factors, which jointly determined the organization of the farm, gets to the heart of answering questions concerning the economic role of farm children. For example, a household may have contained several young children who possessed a comparative advantage in the production of certain goods, such as dairy and poultry products, yet the local climate, soil conditions, and the accessibility of markets may have favored the production of other crops, such as corn or wheat. What crop mix did such a household choose? How did it differ from that of a neighboring household with no children? How did the size of the farms differ? Specifically, did output mix differ among different types of households within and among geographical regions or by farm size?

The answers to these questions will illuminate the economic role of farm children. As the discussion of theories of fertility decline in chapter 1 illustrated, much has been made of how the value of children and their role in the farm economy affected the decline in fertility rates of rural families in the nineteenth century. Regional differences in the economic role of children that corresponded to differences in regional fertility rates can be identified by statistically testing the relationships among household composition, farm size, and output mix. Any inquiry focusing on the value of farm children must consider the economic role they played in the household. If differences in the value of children existed among regions, then the possibility that children performed different tasks in different regions must be considered. The story of the economic role of women and children in the farm household cannot be considered complete without an attempt at determining the tasks they performed on the farm. Still, the allocation of labor on a family farm was not the same as in a corporate factory, where each worker often has a well-defined set of specific tasks. Narrative evidence leads us to suspect that while a division of labor existed in farm households, during certain periods, such as harvest, most family members probably did whatever they could whenever it needed to be done. How can we determine the tasks farm children performed more than a hundred years ago?

Contemporaries witnessed children performing certain tasks and recorded their observations for posterity. This type of information yields clues but does not fulfill the data requirements necessary to statistically test hypotheses concerning the economic role or value of farm children. The next best thing to knowing what children actually did would be to know what farm tasks were performed by children. This can be indirectly determined by first dividing the farms into groups based on the regions and on the household structure and family life cycle stages defined above, and then analyzing the differences in the output portfolios of these groups. Second, estimate the share of gross farm revenue coming from various types of output, and arrange the output into categories according to the type of labor that narrative evidence shows to be most responsible for its production. The estimates of gross revenue from chapter 2 are divided into five categories, based on the type of work required and the household labor most likely responsible for its production.

The first category of output is field crops, including corn and the small grains: wheat, barley, oats, rye, and buckwheat. The second category consists of dairy products, such as butter, cheese, and fluid milk; poultry and eggs; orchard crops; and vegetables, potatoes, and other market-garden products. The third category is increases in the value of the farm from improvements, rising land prices, and the rental value of the house and other structures. The fourth category consists of livestock production, including hay, slaughtered livestock, and increases in the value of livestock. The final category includes all other goods, such as home manufactures. These categories represent the division of labor among household members identified by contemporaries. Men and older boys worked at field crops and land clearing. Women generally produced the market-garden and dairy products, as well as those in the all-else category. Women also supervised children, who specialized in milking, churning, and the production of the truck-farming products. Livestock products seem to have been a joint venture. Men harvested the hay and corn that provided feed, but women and children handled much of the actual feeding. Men butchered the livestock and sheared the sheep, but women processed the meat and spun the wool.

In the Northeast dairy and truck-farm products made up on average 50 percent of the gross farm revenue on yeoman farms, more than twice the percentage of any other category (table 3.3). Northeastern yeomen also derived a larger percentage of income from livestock than did farmers in the other two regions: 21 percent in the Northeast, versus 15 percent in the Midwest and 19 percent on the Frontier. Field crops and gains from land combined made up 26 percent of northeastern gross farm revenue, with the rest (3 percent) coming from all other goods. Midwestern owner-operated farms received more equal shares of their gross revenue from field crops (30 percent), dairy and truck-farm products (29 percent), land (22 percent), and livestock (15) than did those in the Northeast. The proportion of income derived from various categories on frontier farms resembled those of the Midwest: dairy products made up 33 percent of total revenue, with field crops contributing 23 percent, and land and livestock 21 and 19 percent, respectively.

By definition, tenant farms derived considerably less income from land than yeoman farms. For this reason, they have been separated from owners and part-owners in the tables. The estimation of the marketable surplus in appendix A shows that tenant farmers put more resources into the production of field crops than did yeomen farmers. This observation becomes clearer when the proportion of income from various sources for tenants is considered. Other than income from land, the greatest difference between tenants' and owners' income consisted of the percentage derived from field crops. In each region, tenants received a percentage of income from wheat, corn, and other cereals roughly equal to a third more than owner-operators received from these crops. Although owner-operated farms provided from 20 percent

Table 3.3 Life Cycle Stage and Percentage of Gross Revenue per Farm from Various Sources by Region, 1860

Life Cycle Stage	Cereals & Corn		Dairy, Poultry, & Market Garden		Land & Capital Improvements		Hay & Livestock		All Else	
	Owners	Tenants	Owners	Tenants	Owners	Tenants	Owners	Tenants	Owners	Tenants
Northeast										
I	16%	23%	48%	48%	12%	4%	22%	23%	3%	2%
II	15	25	50	46	11	5	21	22	3	2
III	16	26	50	45	12	4	19	23	3	2
IV	14	23	50	50	10	2	22	19	4	5
V	14	24	50	45	11	2	22	29	2	1
All Farms	15	24	50	46	11	4	21	23	3	2
Midwest										
I	31%	39%	29%	32%	23%	7%	14%	16%	2%	3%
II	30	42	29	30	21	4	15	17	3	4
III	30	46	29	29	22	4	16	16	3	3
IV	28	47	29	27	24	4	16	16	3	2
V	27	35	29	38	24	10	17	16	3	1
All Farms	30	41	29	31	22	5	15	16	3	3
Frontier										
I	22%	31%	32%	35%	25%	3%	17%	29%	4%	3%
II	23	28	34	40	21	4	19	25	4	3
III	24	36	32	31	20	2	19	26	4	4
IV	23	N.O.	34	N.O.	22	N.O.	19	N.O.	3	N.O.
V	30	N.O.	38	N.O.	16	N.O.	14	N.O.	2	N.O.
All Farms	23	30	33	37	21	3	19	27	4	3

Source: Author's calculation from Bateman and Foust, *Agricultural and Demographic Records*, tape.
Note: N.O. ("no observations") means there were fewer than 10 farms in that category. Shares may not sum to 100% due to rounding.

to 35 percent more revenue than tenant farms, the actual value of grain production was roughly equal. But tenant households contained on average fewer members and fewer livestock, which reduced on-farm consumption, so that tenants had a larger marketable surplus in grain than did owners.[8]

Since Adam Smith, specialization and division of labor have been associated with increasing economic efficiency. Historians of U.S. agriculture have long argued that commercialization led to increased specialization.[9] One index of regional specialization in production can be derived by summing the squares of the mean percentages of total output for each category in table 3.3. A resulting index of 1.00 would mean that all revenues came from a single category, with smaller numbers representing more diversification.[10] By this measure northeastern farms specialized the most, with an index of 0.33 (0.32 for tenants). Midwestern farms came in second at 0.25 (0.29 for tenants), followed closely by frontier farms at 0.24 (0.30 for tenants). So specialization, at least as measured here, decreased as one moved westward, though the output mix in the Midwest closely resembled that of the Frontier. In addition, appendix A shows that commercialization, as measured by the ratio of surplus production to total production, also decreased as one moved westward. These findings support the traditional view of the relation between commercialization and specialization.[11]

Perhaps the most startling thing about table 3.3 is the almost total lack of variation in the portfolio shares among life cycle stages within each region, particularly with respect to owner-operated farms. By definition the composition of the household varies over the family life cycle. Yet in most cases the share of gross revenue from a given source varies less than a couple of percentage points among life cycle stages within any particular region. But eyeballing the data in this way hardly constitutes hypothesis testing, and we want to test whether the observed differences are statistically significant.

To answer this question two sets of tests must be performed: first, tests for the differences between regions for a given life cycle stage; second, tests for the differences among life cycle stages within each region. If no statistically significant difference existed in output mix over the life cycle within a particular region, but such a difference did exist between regions, it would suggest that the role Chayanov assigned to climate, soil type, or access to markets dominated household structure in the determination of output mix. In other words, household structure in general and children in particular played a subordinate role to location in determining the organization of the farm. Such a result would further indicate that studies emphasizing the economic role or value of children should not focus on their value in producing a particular combination of outputs.

On the other hand, if a statistically significant difference existed among the output mix of farms over the life cycle within a region, but no such difference existed in the output mix of households of the same life cycle stage in different regions, the result would support Chayanov's contention that the composition of the household played a dominant role in the determination of output mix and that children performed some specific tasks associated with a particular output mix. Such a result would indicate that studies focusing on the economic value of children should emphasize the opportunities to use child labor in the production of certain types of output or economic activities. Although these tests cannot measure either the presence or the lack of causality between crop mix and household composition, they do show whether or not households with children produced the same mix of output regardless of region.

The distribution of the proportion of farm output coming from various sources represents an independent multinomial distribution. The comparison of such distributions among farms of different life cycle stages or farms located in different regions involves testing the null hypothesis that any two were the same.[12] Thus, the alternative hypothesis is that the output mixes were different. The test statistic used to test the null hypothesis follows a chi-square distribution.[13] With output divided into the five different categories, each test has four ($i - 1$, where $i = 5$ is the number of different categories of output) degrees of freedom.

For owner-operated farms, two-thirds of the results from testing the output mix of the same life cycle stage among different regions yielded statistically significant test statistics. A statistically significant test statistic means the null hypothesis that the two types of farms had on average the same output mix must be rejected. (Appendix B contains the results of these tests.) In every case the difference between northeastern and midwestern farms yielded a significant test statistic at the 5 percent or less level. In every case the difference between the northeastern and frontier farms was also significant at the 5 percent or less level. In no case did a statistically significant difference exist between midwestern and frontier farms. In other words, the output mix of northeastern farms differed at every stage of the life cycle from those in the Midwest or on the Frontier at the same life cycle stage, but the same cannot be said when the latter two regions were compared to one another.

Compare these results with those obtained from testing the difference between the crop mixes of farms within the same region but at different stages of the household life cycle. The results are even more striking than those from testing for differences among regions. No two distributions of output within any region differed from one another to a statistically significant degree. Taken together, the results from these two sets of tests indicate that the output mix of antebellum farms was strongly associated with the region in which the farms were located. In spite of the results from comparing midwestern and frontier farms, the evidence strongly supports the hypothesis that output mix varied more among regions than among life cycle stages of the household. Broadly speaking, the same results hold for tenant farms, though northeastern and frontier farms did not differ among tenants as they did among owners.[14]

These results point up the futility of searching for some unique economic role for children based on the production of a particular group of products or category of output. While the identification of such roles offers important information for understanding the economics of the farm household, it does not lead to an economic explanation of fertility behavior. Scholars of the nineteenth-century fertility decline have argued that families found the labor of children particularly valuable in the farm-making and land-clearing activities of the frontier. This argument implies that on average, families with children should have specialized in those activities. Yet in chapter 2 we saw overwhelming evidence presented by contemporaries that children specialized in activities more likely to be performed in more settled agriculture. Furthermore, the results from the statistical tests just discussed show that within each region families with only young children or young children and teenagers produced an output mix in the same proportion as young (and old) couples with no children in the household. Within each region families with no children produced output in the same proportions as those with only young children, as well as those with teenagers. The conclusion to be drawn from these results is that children probably did whatever they could to help out whenever it needed to be done, and the same may be said of adults as well.

What explains the contradiction between much of the narrative evidence reported in the previous chapter and the empirical results discussed here? To answer this question, consider the household as an institutional arrangement that organizes the activities of its members. Parents supervise household production and have at their disposal different types of labor and other resources. The farm household produces a large number of different types of output, and it allocates inputs such that the marginal productivity of each equalizes across all possible activities. It may well have been, as contemporaries noted, that women and children rarely performed field work, concentrating on tasks in and around the farmhouse. But since the farm was a multi-product organization, the family often shifted women and children to "men's work" (and vice versa) in times of pressing need—typically at harvest, but possibly at planting and other times as well. Women and children may have been much less productive than adult men when it came to the heavy labor required for clearing land or harvesting grain, but they often helped nonetheless. Their labor would have been particularly valuable in these activities during the most crucial labor demand times.

Women and children were not the only household workers to help with other tasks from time to time. Men and boys often had to help out with the churning, canning, and tending to the garden when these tasks overburdened the women. Contemporaries claimed that men disliked dairying, considering it "women's work," but the value of dairy products on farms with access to urban markets induced men to actively participate in the operation of the dairy, and the same can be said of market-garden products. Even though a general division of labor was in effect throughout much of the year and across much of the North, during peak demand periods, when a particular product demanded immediate attention, or when local economic conditions dictated, everyone pitched in and contributed in whatever way they could, and work activities became less easily identified by age or gender.

Of course the results reported here could be biased by differences in other variables. For example, farm size varied over the life cycle of the family and, like location, helped determine the output mix. Farm size played an important role in crop mix in the cotton South, where in 1860 the share of total crop revenue coming from cotton was roughly two and a half times greater on the largest plantations (those with fifty or more slaves) than on farms with no slaves.[15] The sources of revenue could have varied by farm size in the North as well. Table 3.2 shows that total farm size changed over the life cycle of the family; therefore, the source of revenue could have changed with farm size as well. In particular, increases in the share of output from land increased with the size of the farm (table 3.4), suggesting that output mix differed as farms became larger.

To analyze the effect of size on output mix, I divided the farms into five different groups based on "spikes" in the size distribution. The spikes could be found at 40, 80, 120, and 160 acres in the Midwest, and 50, 100, 150, and 200 acres in the Northeast.[16] These spikes represent the institutional arrangements under which pioneers settled each region. Although the "6 × 6" 36-square-mile township originated in colonial New England, the Northeast had no system for disposing of the land like that specified in the Northwest Ordinance, and the farms clustered around multiples of 50 acres. In the lands beyond the Appalachians, however, the Northwest Ordinance and subsequent public land legislation established the terms of settlement. The minimum purchase of one section or 640 acres (1 square mile) lasted until 1800, when it was cut to 320 acres. In 1804 the minimum became 160 acres; in 1820 it was cut to 80 acres; and in 1832 a pioneer family could obtain a minimum of 40 acres of the public domain at a Land Office auction. Thus, the farms are divided into a small group (0–40 acres), three medium-size groups (41–80, 81–120, and 121–160 acres), and a large group (160 or more acres), each containing a spike in the distribution of farm size.

The distribution of revenue coming from various classes of products shows a little more variation by farm size than by household type, particularly among tenant farms, but in general output mix still seems to have been most influenced by regional location rather than farm size. Families in the middle stages of the life cycle tended to have larger farms, which we would expect given the pattern of wealth accumulation found in table 3.2. If the output mix of farms of different sizes displayed a statistically significant difference within a particular region, and if no difference existed between the output mix of farms of the same size in different regions, it would suggest that larger farms had a different crop mix than smaller ones, regardless of region. Such a result might have been associated with the difference in household structure or life cycle stage. Southern farms displayed this characteristic with respect to cotton production, with the larger farms growing a significantly larger proportion of cotton than smaller ones. Such a result would indicate that studies focusing on the economic value of children should emphasize the wealth accumulation and scale of agriculture associated with middle stages of the family life cycle. In this way children might have played a distinct role in determining the type of output produced

Table 3.4 Farm Size and Percentage of Gross Revenue per Farm from Various Sources by Region, 1860

Farm Size (Acres)	Cereals & Corn		Dairy, Poultry, & Market Garden		Land & Capital Improvements		Hay & Livestock		All Else	
	Owners	Tenants	Owners	Tenants	Owners	Tenants	Owners	Tenants	Owners	Tenants
Northeast										
0–40	14%	23%	52%	51%	10%	1%	22%	24%	2%	1%
41–80	16	23	50	49	10	3	21	23	3	2
81–120	16	25	50	47	11	4	20	22	3	2
121–160	15	27	49	40	12	6	21	25	3	2
161+	15	25	47	45	14	7	20	21	4	3
All Farms	15	24	50	46	11	4	21	23	3	2
Midwest										
0–40	29	40%	38%	33%	15%	1%	14%	15%	2%	4%
41–80	29	45	31	30	19	5	16	16	3	2
81–120	30	40	29	29	22	6	15	20	3	3
121–160	31	39	25	32	24	10	15	16	3	3
161+	30	38	24	27	27	13	15	17	3	3
All Farms	30	41	29	31	22	5	15	16	3	3
Frontier										
0–40	20%	37%	42%	27%	14%	2%	20%	28%	4%	6%
41–80	19	34	36	36	22	4	18	23	5	3
81–120	24	32	32	31	23	8	18	25	4	4
121–160	27	26	28	43	23	3	20	27	3	2
161+	28	30	28	33	23	5	18	30	3	2
All Farms	23	30	33	37	21	3	19	27	4	3

Source: Author's calculation from Bateman and Foust, Agricultural and Demographic Records, tape.
Note: Shares may not sum to 100% due to rounding.

on the farm. On the other hand, if no difference existed among the output shares of farms of different size within a region, but a difference could be found among farms of the same size but located in different regions, then that would reinforce the conclusion that climate, soil type, and access to urban markets dominated household structure when it came to crop choice.

For owners and part-owners, the overwhelming majority of all farms, the results correspond closely to those found for life cycle stage. (The statistical results are shown in appendix B). In almost every case comparing the Northeast with either the Midwest or Frontier the differences are statistically significant. When we compare the distributions within a given region, however, in no case are the differences statistically significant. In other words, regardless of farm size, farmers in the Northeast received income from a different mix of products than did farmers in the other two regions. Farmers in the Midwest derived income from the various categories of crops in the same proportion as did those on the Frontier. Within each region, yeomen farmers derived revenue from products in the same proportion regardless of farm size. A difference can be found among large and small tenant farms within each region, but in a smaller proportion of cases than is found between regions. The difference between the results for tenants and owners within each region stems from the lack of returns from land on tenant farms and the more specialized nature of tenant farming, as noted already. Owners derived a larger proportion of gross revenue from land by definition, and they maintained more diversified crop portfolios at every scale of farm operation than tenants; thus, tenants show more difference within each region than owners.

Many scholars who have studied regional differences in nineteenth-century fertility rates have concluded that women and children played distinct roles in the farm economy, and that a relation existed between this and the fertility rate. This conclusion implies that households with different types of labor—that is, laborers of different ages and gender—would tend to differ in their choice of output mix. In fact, this conclusion cannot be drawn from the evidence presented here for antebellum northern farms. The determining factor in output selection was more likely to have been regionally related variables, such as climate, soil type, or market proximity, and not household composition or farm size. Northeastern farms, located near urban markets and not well suited for extensive field crops, derived more than 50 percent of their gross revenues from dairy and truck-farming products. Farms in the Old Northwest and the trans-Mississippi frontier, located on soils ideal

for corn and wheat, bulk crops with relatively long storage lives, derived revenue in more equal proportions from field crops, dairy and
market-garden products, gains from land, and livestock production
than did those in the Northeast. These farmers grew grain for market
and produced perishables for home consumption. The relative sparse-
ness of settlement encouraged a more diversified strategy until the
emergence of markets made specialization profitable.

The strategies adopted by northern farmers depended heavily on
the location of their farms, and this conclusion leads away from explaining fertility behavior by studying the productive activities of farm
children. But how were farm strategies manifested in other ways? The
rise of more efficient means of transportation played an indispensable
role in the development of U.S. agriculture. The public financing required by large-scale transportation networks politically linked the
rural North and the development of internal improvements such as
canals and railroads. Despite the views of the late-nineteenth century
Populists, farmers initially welcomed the canal and later the iron horse.
These improvements taking place beyond the Appalachians forced
northeastern farmers into the dairy, hay, and truck farming activities
discussed in chapter 2. Politically the Whigs, dominated by Henry
Clay's American System, represented these aspirations in the 1830s
and 1840s, though the protectionist and probusiness aspects of the Whig
platform kept the Midwest politically diverse until the compromise
over slavery in the territories collapsed in the 1850s.

The ease of access to western land and improvements in transportation allowed products from the Ohio and Mississippi valleys to
compete with those from the Northeast. The differences in crop portfolios among regions that have been presented here reflect the outcome
by 1860 of this competition, which had been going on for decades. As
with other forms of economic conflict, this one could not be kept from
the political arena. Throughout the antebellum era regional conflicts
flared. Tariffs, national banking, publicly subsidized transportation
projects, the public lands, states' rights, and slavery all involved regional conflict. The Free Soil movement had an economic dimension
in the acquisition of western land and the proliferation of western
products, pitting East against West. But the South's intransigence over
the expansion of slavery into the Kansas Territory united abolitionists
and Unionists, Yankee farmers and prairie yeomen. The North-South
conflict effectively overwhelmed the differences between East and
West.

By 1860 most of the northeasterners who remained in farming

realized that no amount of political agitation could block the opening of the continent to agricultural settlement, and they pursued their comparative (regional) advantage in dairying and truck farming. All of these events affected the organization of farm production, crop mix, and the economic roles and value of women and children in agriculture. The results reported in this chapter demonstrate that soil type, climate, and proximity to markets determined the organization of farm production, rather than life cycle stage, household composition, or farm size. Thus it seems futile to look for a unique economic niche that made children inherently more valuable to their parents in the production of one product or another, since household members performed whatever tasks they could whenever those tasks needed to be done. Despite these conclusions, the findings do not imply that economic models of fertility decline are useless. They merely indicate that the quest for a model to explain fertility must go beyond the roles children played as producers of specific products. A great deal of research has been done in recent years to explain fertility decline as a function of the intergenerational transfers of wealth through *inter vivos* transfers or bequests. Much of this work, however, has fallen back on the notion of the unique economic role of children in the various regions, claiming, for example, that children were particularly valuable in the clearing of western land.

I argue instead that the role of children as producers does not support the bequest argument. If children proved most valuable in production in regions of high fertility, as many scholars have assumed, then why would elaborate theories of bequests be needed to arrive at an economic explanation of differences in fertility rates? Rather, the *lack* of unique regional roles in production makes the bequest argument so important to an explanation of fertility decline. The fact that one cannot identify a particular output mix for a given household composition does not mean that differences did not exist among regions in the value of women or children as producers. Further, while it certainly says nothing about the relationship between children and bequests, it does eliminate a particular line of argument going back to those nineteenth-century observers who saw women and children in separate roles from adult men. The more interesting question now seems to be not what household members did, but how valuable they were regardless of what they did.

Children provided labor services to parents through the production of farm output. They also were a potential source of old age security. Parents supplied their children with upkeep until the children left home, and often also provided either an endowment to start adult life or a bequest upon the death of one or both parents. In addition, differences in the value of adult labor, that of women in particular, influenced the amount of time parents could spend on children. Each of these factors and the variables that determined them influenced fertility.

CHAPTER FOUR

The Economic Value of Women and Children in Northern Agriculture

During the antebellum era, the small-scale family farms that composed the agricultural sector in the North employed a substantial amount of child labor, as did early manufacturing establishments in the Northeast. Over the past 130 years, the share of the labor force in agriculture fell from more than 50 percent to less than 3 percent; mandatory school attendance through the middle teens became universal; and labor laws prohibited the large-scale employment of children in many occupations, including most of the manufacturing sector.[1] In addition, the provision of employee pension plans, annuities, and social security meant that parents decreased their reliance on children for old age security. A shift in the ethics of society away from viewing children as "best seen and not heard" and toward an appreciation of their rights as citizens accompanied these legislative and market changes. Together all of these changes contributed to a decrease in the value of children as producers and as providers of old age security.

The work of adults changed considerably over time as well. Both men and women worked predominantly in agriculture before the Civil War, but records of the labor market activities of men considerably outweigh those of women and children. Men more often sold their labor as hired hands than did women, though women domestics constituted a sizable proportion of all women workers. After "farmer," "domestic service" dominated all other occupations of rural women reporting jobs in 1860.[2] Children often worked for wages as well, but unfortunately little direct evidence exists concerning the value of the activities of either women or children. Nineteenth-century agricultural journals and the correspondence of contemporaries contain occasional comments concerning the wages of children and domestics, but relatively few reliable wage data comparable to those available for men remain from the antebellum era. The sources that reported earnings for women and children claimed a hired boy earned on average from $4 to $8 per month during the 1850s in Illinois and Indiana, depending on the season for which he was hired, his age, and his experience. By the time he reached his late teens, a young man could earn $1.00 a day and $1.25 or more at harvest. Girls and domestics typically earned from 50¢ to 75¢ on the dollar compared to boys and hired hands in the same region, though on occasion they earned nearly as much as the men.[3] This evidence, though valuable in supplying information to compare estimates derived from more rigorous statistical techniques, clearly provides insufficient data for the testing of hypotheses concerning the relative value of women and children. An economic explanation of differences in birthrates among the different regions of the North requires such estimates.

Better evidence of the value of women and children employed in nineteenth-century northern agriculture contributes to a better understanding of history in three ways. First, the value of children in different regions helps explain regional differences in rural fertility rates. To the extent that children provided productive services to their parents, the greater their value the more children one would expect parents to desire. Second, the results provide valuable information about the economics of farming in the antebellum North. Estimating the value of women and children tells us about their economic roles in the household. Third, the results enhance our understanding of other agrarian economies. The transformation of the U.S. economy from agriculture to manufacturing and services offers lessons for developing countries that still have large primary sectors.

To derive the contribution to the production process of a particular input, economists typically use statistical techniques, multiple regression being the primary tool. These methods provide estimates of the parameters of a *production function*—that is, the mathematical representation of the technology describing the relationship between inputs (such as women, children, and implements) and outputs (such as corn, hogs, and milk). But the specification of production technology generally consists of highly aggregated inputs, such as capital and labor, and obstructs the disaggregation of these inputs. Yet the issues outlined in the previous chapters demand such disaggregation. Further, estimation using the standard production functions requires nonzero values

75

for each input for each household, presenting a further obstacle to estimating the value of specific types of labor. This requirement limits the degrees of freedom available for estimation and discards information with the omitted observations. The following multiple regression technique allows us to avoid these problems.

The agricultural production on the small-scale family farms that marked the antebellum North typically displayed the quality economists refer to as constant returns to scale, meaning that if a farmer doubled all of the inputs, such as land, labor, and capital, then output would double as well.[4] Likewise, if a farmer halved all of the inputs, then output would be halved as well, and so on. Assuming that the technology of production on the farms in the sample displays this characteristic, then output, Y, of the farm will be allocated among the N inputs, $X_1, \ldots, X_N$, such that the sum of the product of the inputs and their marginal products equals Y.[5] In competitive input markets the marginal contribution of labor should equal its wage. As noted, however, information concerning the wages, $w = (w_1, \ldots, w_N)$, for all of the inputs is not available. Some wages are known, for instance the wage rates of hired men, but reliable wage data do not exist for women and children. The subset of wages, $w^* = (w_{n+1}, \ldots, w_N)$, including those for women and children, captures the marginal contribution of the different types of household labor. Their contribution can be estimated by subtracting from total output the returns that go to the other n inputs, such as land, capital, and livestock. The value of output going to household labor constitutes the remainder; call it Y^*.[6]

Strictly speaking, productivity represents a measure of output per unit of time. Since little information has survived concerning the amounts of time worked by individuals of different age or gender, this method of deriving estimates of the value of various types of labor does not yield direct measures of productivity. Although it might be reasonable to assume that individuals of the same age and gender worked the same amounts of time within a particular region, differences between regions may well have been present, and comparisons of the value of labor between regions and different categories of labor should be made with this point in mind. To reflect the absence of information on the time input, the estimates derived below have been labeled *marginal contribution to farm output* rather than *marginal product*, though in fact the two should be similar.

Although much of American social history contrasts the noble yeoman with his supposedly more crass counterpart in mercantile or industrial pursuits—a style derived directly from Jefferson, but long fashionable in western intellectual circles—the farmer, whether owner or tenant, essentially stood as an entrepreneur. Owner-operators, as capitalists, accrued their net product from farm production and capital gains from farm wealth after compensating other inputs. Tenants, as renters only, did not receive capital gains or rents from the farm itself. In both cases, however, the output not allocated to labor and other inputs shows up as a residual measure that can be used to compute rates of profit and can be compared to other estimates of profitability as a check on the validity of the results.[7]

Chapter 2 contained the estimation of gross farm revenue, but in order to derive the share of gross farm revenue going to household labor, the value of the known inputs or the returns to other factors must be subtracted. After subtracting the returns to other factors, the value of farm output going to household labor and the profit or quasi-rent going to the farm owner or tenant remain. This profit represents a return above the opportunity wage the operator could expect as a laborer.[8] Labor received the largest share of farm income on the Frontier (84 percent) and the smallest share in the Northeast (69 percent), with midwestern labor receiving 77 percent (table 4.1). These figures

Table 4.1 Allocation of Northern Farm Income by Factor of Production and Region, 1860

Returns to Factors of Production	North	Northeast	Midwest	Frontier
Feed, seed, and depreciation	$147.58	$165.27	$153.61	$ 67.44
Rental payments (tenants only)	189.65	308.85	135.09	54.02
Returns to land, capital, and wages	130.69	211.70	86.85	67.26
Sum of returns to factors other than household labor	303.79 (25.91%)	505.35 (31.04%)	211.07 (22.96%)	123.05 (15.86%)
Returns to household labor	868.64 (74.09%)	1,122.69 (68.96%)	708.08 (77.04%)	732.42 (84.14%)
Gross revenue	1,172.43	1,628.04	919.15	775.74

Sources: Tables 2.1–2.3; appendix A; and Lee A. Craig, "The Value of Household Labor in Antebellum Northern Agriculture," *Journal of Economic History* 51 (March 1991): 67–82.
Note: Figures in parentheses represent the percentage of gross revenue going to that factor of production. Gross revenue figures differ slightly from table 2.4 due to rounding.

reflect the more land- and capital-intensive farming in the Northeast relative to the other regions. Farmers spent more on livestock feed, hired hands, rent, and depreciation in the Northeast than in the other two regions, all indications of the proximity of markets and the prevalence of "scientific" farming in the Northeast. Settled agriculture was a relatively less labor-intensive activity than frontier agriculture. Yet the total dollar value of the returns to household labor still remained 50 percent above that of midwestern or frontier farms. Given this information one would expect that, other things being equal, household labor would have been more valuable in the Northeast than elsewhere.

The equation or model to be estimated identifies seven population groups, broken down by age and gender. Children were grouped into ages zero through six and seven through twelve. After age thirteen the labor force has been divided into boys and girls to capture the distinctly different roles they played in the farm household, beginning with adolescence. Dividing the children into these groups results from the observation that among preteen children little difference existed in their activities according to gender, and that children began "purposeful" economic activity around the ages of seven to ten. As a boy, Laura Ingalls's future husband, Almanzo Wilder, began helping with chores before his ninth birthday; although he and his sister, who was a couple of years older, had some separate chores, they often worked side by side around the farm. On the other hand, Almanzo's teenage brother and sister never worked together. His teenaged brother, while sharing with Almanzo the daily chore of tending the livestock, most often did the work of an adult, and their teenaged sister worked almost exclusively in and around the home with her mother. The experience of the Wilder family typified that of many northern farm households, though as noted in chapters 2 and 3, most household members probably helped with all of the chores at one time or another. In the South slave children began work around the same age as other farm children, and in contemporary developing countries children begin work between the ages of seven and ten as well.[9] In addition to this narrative evidence, no statistically significant difference could be found between the value of boys and girls under the age of thirteen.

As noted in chapter 2, except during periods of particularly heavy labor demand, such as harvest, women and preteen children performed field work less frequently than men, who in turn were unlikely to help much with household chores; for this reason, as with teens, I have separated adult women from men. In addition, men were divided into those age nineteen through fifty-four and those age fifty-five and older.

78

Disaggregating men in this way provides two advantages. First, it allows one to compare the contribution of prime-age men (those age nineteen through fifty-four) living in the household with the recorded wages of hired hands, most of whom were men in this age group; this comparison provides a check on the methodology employed to derive estimates of the contributions of women and children. If the results from the estimation of the marginal contribution of men age nineteen through fifty-four turn out to be close to market wages, then one can have confidence in the results for women and children. Second, dividing men into two age groups allows one to check for evidence of an individual life cycle. As workers age, beyond some point their productivity falls off. In the case of nineteenth-century farmers, a drop in their contribution to farm output may be due to infirmity or semi-retirement. Although the value of women's labor could have changed with age as well, little information exists on either the ages or wage rates of hired women for comparison; therefore, they are not disaggregated.

The model also includes a variable capturing the effect of farm size on farm income. The process of accumulation of wealth (primarily land) over time subject to the competitive forces of the market meant that the most successful farmers were those whose farms survived and grew. Although the process of separating out unsuccessful farmers occurred over time, at any point in time those who had demonstrated skill most likely farmed larger farms; thus, farm size captures the potential returns to the better management found on larger farms.[10] This variable takes the value of 1 if a farm consisted of more than 80 acres.[11]

In general the marginal contribution to farm output by children and teenage girls did not statistically differ across regions (table 4.2).[12] Children under the age of seven did not significantly contribute to output in any region. In the Midwest, however, children between seven and twelve contributed about $28 and teenage girls around $40. In other words, children under the age of thirteen and teenage girls contributed the equivalent of one and one-half to two months' wages of a hired man in the Midwest, but in the Northeast and on the Frontier children contributed less, and the coefficients were not statistically significant.[13] It is important that children and teenage girls did not contribute much to market output relative to men in any region. Teenage girls contributed the most in the Midwest, but even here they contributed only 22 percent as much to farm output as did men.

Women contributed twice as much to the value of farm output in

Table 4.2 Dollar Value of Household Labor in Northern Agriculture by Region, 1860

	North (standard error)	Northeast (standard error)	Midwest (standard error)	Frontier (standard error)
Profit	$169.26	$234.55	$164.85	$117.57
	(29.48)	(66.79)	(26.83)	(49.61)
Children				
(age 0–6)	−19.80	−20.82	8.59	−6.41
	(7.39)	(18.29)	(6.40)	(12.43)
Children	16.38	22.81	27.76	27.12
(age 7–12)	(10.52)	(25.91)	(8.87)	(18.96)
Teenage females	22.01	22.95	39.75	17.53
	(16.06)	(37.91)	(13.79)	(29.74)
Teenage males	58.31	111.03	47.57	49.03
	(15.03)	(35.95)	(12.74)	(28.84)
Adult females	152.63	154.08	70.25	147.28
	(13.49)	(28.04)	(12.63)	(30.04)
Adult males	229.09	294.77	186.44	193.66
(age 19–54)	(16.69)	(38.88)	(14.89)	(26.84)
Adult males	175.60	145.95	121.94	135.44
(55 and older)	(24.65)	(48.52)	(24.17)	(55.07)
Farm size	269.26	422.52	223.61	221.98
Dummy variable	(18.83)	(44.45)	(16.76)	(31.11)
N	8,496	3,130	4,347	1,019

Source: Craig, "Value of Household Labor," pp. 67–82.
Note: The dependent variable is the value of labor's output from table 5.2. The estimation technique was generalized least squares.

80

the Northeast and on the Frontier as they did in the Old Northwest. In the Northeast their contribution approximated the wage of a hired hand for seven to eight months, which represents the standard contract length for hired hands at that time. So having a woman in the household year-round contributed on average as much to the value of market output as hiring a farmhand from planting through harvest. The ratio of the value of the output of a woman to that of a man reached 0.52 in the Northeast, depending on the length of contract for hired labor. This ratio compares favorably with the 0.44–0.52 figures reported elsewhere for the ratio of women's to men's wages in other sectors of the northeastern economy in 1850.[14] These results suggest that the ratio of men's to women's wages had been roughly equalized among sectors by the eve of the Civil War. But it should be kept in mind when interpreting these coefficients that they capture only market production and the contribution to increases in farm value. They omit the value of domestic production or housework. In fact, if one imputes the wage of a full-time domestic to a woman, then the market value of the total contribution to the household by a woman exceeds that by a man in every region.

For teenage boys a discontinuity existed across regions. In the Midwest and on the Frontier their marginal contribution was not quite twice that of children age seven through twelve in the same regions, around $48. In the Northeast, however, the value jumped to $111. The marginal contribution of men age nineteen through fifty-four almost equaled the average wage for a hired hand working around nine months in the Midwest and on the Frontier, while in the Northeast it was slightly more than the wages of a hired hand employed for a full twelve months. Although these estimates would have been toward the high end of the length of the standard contract in the antebellum North, it is not unrealistic to expect that the contribution of those workers living in the household year-round, the majority of whom were farmers and their sons, surpassed the contribution of a hired hand who worked only part of the year. Even in seasons other than planting and harvesting, work needed to be performed. Corn had to be shelled, grain threshed, and livestock fed and cared for; maintenance of implements and other such work would have contributed to market output indirectly by making subsequent activity more productive. A life cycle effect can be seen in the decline in the contribution of men after age fifty-five, though the results for older men do not tell us whether this decline was due to physical deterioration, voluntary semiretirement, or some combination of the two.

The profit coefficients seem reasonable as well, yielding profit rates that compare favorably to those obtained by others.[15] For both owner-operated and tenant farms the profit rate would have been 10.4 percent in the Northeast and 9.7 percent in the Midwest. While these figures are below recent estimates of 12.6 percent in the Northeast and 12.1 percent in the Midwest, they are close and possess the correct relative magnitude.[16] In addition, unlike other estimates, mine impute a wage to the labor of household members other than men; therefore, one would expect the profit rates calculated from table 4.2 to be lower than those that do not contain compensation for household labor. This would explain some if not all of the difference in our results.

As noted above, the farm size variable can be viewed as a proxy for measures of the quality of management. If farmers who owned larger farms provided better management, then they should have earned a return above the mean. As expected, this variable has a significant effect in each region.[17] Northeastern farmers managing more than 80 acres realized a premium of one and a half times the annual wages of a hired hand. Due to the larger number of improved relative to unimproved acres, northeastern farms enjoyed a higher premium from larger size than elsewhere, but on average for the entire North, farmers received a substantial premium for managing a larger farm, equaling roughly twelve months' wages for a hired hand.

These estimates provide systematic evidence concerning the relative contribution to farm output of women, children, and men of different ages. Until now there has been some evidence concerning the wages of hired boys, good wage data for men, and a reliable set of profit rate estimates for northern agriculture. The narrative sources of these data confirm the reliability of my estimates. The implicit wage rate of teenage boys in the Old Northwest matches the figures cited in the periodicals of the day and the correspondence of contemporaries; the coefficients for prime-age men correspond with the wage rate for hired hands; and the profit rates are within a couple of percentage points and have the correct relative magnitude of earlier estimates. In addition to these checks, sensitivity tests with respect to the calculation of gross revenue and the definition of men's labor yield results consistent with expectations.[18] Therefore, we can have confidence in the estimates of the contribution to farm output of children's and women's labor.

The differences in the type of agriculture practiced among the regions explain the differences in the relative contributions of various types of farm labor. This interpretation arises from results derived using several definitions of output. Northeastern farms had more improved acreage and capital to work with and were in general closer to off-farm markets than western farms, all of which enhanced the market value of any effort farm laborers put forth. Contemporary commentators noted the relatively large quantity of structures and high quality of the homes in the Northeast compared to the Midwest and Frontier. They also noted that women and children were more likely to perform field work and land-clearing activities in areas in which labor was relatively scarce—that is, the less settled regions. Northeastern farms had more than twice as large a share of the total farm value in structures as elsewhere, but the share of the increase in the value of the farm from improving acreage and clearing land in the Midwest was nearly double that in the Northeast. Gains from clearing land made up a greater share of output in the Midwest than in either the Northeast or the Frontier.

Excluding these gains from the value of farm output and once again estimating the regressions in table 4.2 biases downward the contribution of labor in the Midwest relative to other regions; as expected, the contribution of both teenage groups fell significantly in the midwestern estimates, but those for the Northeast changed little. More important, the ratios of the contributions of teenage boys and girls changed little.[19] The results with capital gains excluded indicate that young children still contributed more output in the Midwest than in the other two regions. Although the estimation yielded a higher coefficient for children age seven through twelve in the Northeast than in the Midwest, that northeastern coefficient was not significant. The coefficient for teenage girls in the Midwest was no longer significant, indicating a land-clearing role for girls that was absent in the other two regions.[20] According to my evidence, it appears that in the Northeast teenage girls were largely responsible for the relatively high quality of the home, but in the Midwest they neglected home work for land clearing and crop production. I conclude that teenage boys and girls were more likely to perform the same tasks in the Midwest, namely market production and land clearing, but in the Northeast the boys were more likely to specialize in market production and the girls in household production.[21]

Regional differences in the emphasis placed on dairying show up in this analysis as well. Contemporary commentators noted that northeastern men and boys typically worked in their dairies, but midwesterners, particularly those of southern descent, avoided the task, thinking it "women's work." The narrative evidence in chapter 2 and the empirical results in table 4.1 corroborated these impressions. Dairy products made up the single largest component of farm income in the Northeast and were more important there than in the other two regions: 37 percent in the Northeast, compared to 18 percent and 21 percent in the Midwest and on the Frontier, respectively.[22] Subtracting the value of these products from the total value of farm output and once again estimating the regressions in table 4.2 biases downward the contribution of labor in the Northeast compared to the other two regions. Omitting dairy products from gross revenue causes the coefficient on teenage boys in the Northeast to fall, but not enough to make it smaller than that for the other regions. While teenage boys did contribute significantly to northeastern dairying, it appears that a difference existed in their contribution to output beyond their role in that activity. The greater value of capital, the larger proportion of improved to total acres, and the relative importance of dairying in the Northeast all undoubtedly help explain this result. Likewise, when dairy products are omitted from gross revenue the contribution of women dropped by 58 percent in the Northeast but only by 47 percent and 32 percent in the Midwest and on the Frontier, respectively. The decline in the Northeast highlights the importance of women in the region's dairy industry. In addition, the coefficients for men fell by around 55 percent in the Northeast but only by 26 percent in the Midwest and 24 percent in the Frontier.

Together, these results indicate that fathers, sons, and hired hands took part in the dairy operations in the Northeast to a greater extent than in the Midwest and on the Frontier, just as the narrative evidence would indicate, but that women also contributed a great deal to dairying in the Northeast. The comments of contemporaries may have reflected the value of dairying in the two regions more than any cultural variations between Yankees and others. Further, the results help explain the differences between the contribution of teenage girls and women in the Northeast. As noted, there was a large change in the coefficient for women when dairying was omitted, but no significant change showed up for teenage girls. This result reinforces the earlier interpretation that from the time she reached her teens until adulthood a young woman focused mainly on home production, but afterwards she directed her labor more toward market activity, particularly dairying.

Until now we have known little about the role and contribution of women's and children's labor in antebellum northern agriculture beyond the observations recorded by contemporaries. These estimates provide the first systematic evidence concerning the relative contribution to farm output of women and children. Children between the ages of seven and twelve and teenage girls made their largest contribution in the Old Northwest. In the other two regions their contributions were not significant. Teenage boys, men, and women made their largest contribution in the Northeast. These results contradict the widely held views that children contributed more in the least settled region or that no difference existed between regions. Children and teenagers were more valuable in the production of crops and dairy products in the more settled regions than in the farm-making activities of frontier agriculture. In those areas where children did contribute significantly, young children and teenage girls contributed more to farm output in the extensive agriculture practiced in the woodlands of Ohio and Indiana and the settled part of Illinois than in the more intensive agriculture of the Northeast or the farm-making areas on the Frontier. On the other hand, teenage boys contributed more to farm output in the Northeast than elsewhere.

The results also show that girls must have engaged in some land-clearing activities in the Midwest, but not in the Northeast. This suggests further that teenage boys and girls more frequently performed the same tasks in the Midwest—namely, market production and land clearing—than in the Northeast, where the boys more likely specialized in market production and the girls in household production. Contrary to the comments of contemporaries, these results indicate that women were quite important in northeastern dairy farming. The dairying results also reinforce the conclusion that differences in the contribution of teenage girls and women in the Northeast reflected differences in the degree of market orientation of the work performed by each group.

These results support those from chapter 3 concerning the roles of women and children in the antebellum farm economy. The location of the farm dictated to a large extent the allocation of the household's resources. Regardless of the age, gender, and quantity of household members, climate, soil type, and access to markets determined the mix of outputs, and therefore the members' tasks. Although broadly speaking, men and teenage boys, (including hired hands) primarily handled the responsibilities of planting, cultivating, and harvesting field crops throughout the North, the extent to which they participated in other activities differed among regions. The fact that men and boys were much more likely to participate in dairying in the Northeast than elsewhere reflects the value of dairy products in that region. The findings that children in general, and girls in particular, typically focused their activities on tasks around the home and in the garden and barnyard, but that in the Midwest they participated in farm-making activities to a greater extent than in the Northeast, reflect the importance of different activities in each region.

Knowing what the average child of a certain age or gender contributed to the value of household production is not the same as knowing whether or not they were net assets to their parents. Nor do differences in the marginal contribution to farm output by children among the regions prove that differences in the net value of children varied in the same way. After discounting future returns and accounting for child mortality, what difference remained in the net present value of a child's production at birth among the three regions? How did the value of consumption and the costs of bequests differ among the regions? What were the differences between the value of children in the provision of old age security? The answers to these questions require the calculation of the *net present value of a child at birth*—that is, the lump sum credit or debit parents would have to have realized at the birth of a child to equal the lifetime stream of costs and benefits from raising that child.

Estimating the net present value of a child at birth requires six pieces of information. The *value of the marginal contribution to farm output* captures the child's productive services. The *value of the consumption by household members* measures the inputs into raising a child. *Mortality rates* by age and gender reflect the probability that a child will survive to the next age. The *present value of any bequest* must also be accounted for, as must the *present value of children in the provision of old age security*. Finally, *all future costs and returns* must be discounted.

The first two pieces of information have already been constructed and presented earlier in this book. Table 4.2 presents the estimates of the marginal contribution to farm output by age, gender, and region. Appendix A explains the estimation of the value of consumption by household members. Although no direct way of measuring the value of the time parents put into rearing children exists for the antebellum era, the value of the goods input can be measured. If the value of goods that go into the production of children is less than the value of time that is taken up by rearing children (an assumption supported by contemporary observation), then one can use the value of goods as a lower bound proxy for the value of time. For the calculations below, I used twice the value of consumption to approximate the combination of the goods and time input. One must also account for the costs of mortality. Life tables of the probability that a child of a certain age will survive to the next age have been constructed for various historical settings. Following other scholars researching the demographic behavior of antebellum Americans, I have used "level seven" mortality from the "West" model life tables to determine the probability of a farm child surviving at each age.[23] These life tables yield an expectation of life at birth in the mid thirties and, reflecting the high infant mortality of the day, expectation of life at age one in the low forties.

Any explanation of farm family fertility must come to grips with the role of bequests, and a bequest payment must be explicitly accounted for. (Appendix C presents a model of farm family fertility that explicitly includes bequest payments.) Four aspects of the establishment of a bequest must be addressed before we can consider its specific functional form. First, we must distinguish bequests from *inter vivos* transfers. Second, we must explore the various bequest-funding schemes at parents' disposal. Third, we need to reexamine the underlying motives of the bequest. Finally, we must determine the size of the bequest.

What were labeled *targeted bequests* in chapter 1, following Richard Easterlin and others, in fact closely resemble *inter vivos* transfers— that is, transfers conducted during the life of the transferer, in this case parents. Pure bequests on the other hand are a disposition of property after death, the word *bequest* being derived from *bequeath*, literally, to dispose of property by will. Thus, bequests fit more closely the role of intergenerational transfers in the sense the term is used in the strategic bequest hypothesis. Of course it could have been the case that parents planned a bequest, but made *inter vivos* transfers because their strategic position eroded and a transfer to their children had to be made before old age. Or parents might have planned an *inter vivos* transfer but died unexpectedly, and ended up leaving a bequest. The point is that what appear to be altruistic transfers could in fact be strategic or vice versa.

At first glance, there appears to be a difference between the funding of the two types of bequests. For example, suppose one set of parents wanted to establish their children on a farm of a certain value when the children left home, following the targeted bequest motive, but another set of parents wanted to obtain resources from their children with the promise of a farm of the same value upon the parents' death, following the strategic bequest motive. The funding of these two schemes would seem quite different. But in order for the strategic bequest to be meaningful, the parents who employed it would have had to post a bond of equivalent present value to the bequest. In other words, unless they offered some guarantee of the maintenance of the value of the transfer, they could not have induced their children to uphold their end of the bargain. At the time these parents decided to produce children, they needed to fund an intergenerational transfer. Regardless of the type of bequest they planned, farmers had to establish some type of funding scheme in order to make the promise to their children credible.

One way to fund a bequest would be to set aside a lump sum at the time of a child's birth. This lump sum could be used to purchase adjacent land to be given to the child in the future, or it could be put into some other form of interest-bearing asset. Another method of funding the bequest would have been periodic payments into an account that provided the bequest at some future date. For example, the parents might purchase some land every year; or they might save some money every year and buy land after accumulating a certain amount of money; or they might borrow the money up front, purchase the land, and pay the loan off over time. In all these cases the present value of the bequest would be roughly the same. In this framework, what matters to the farm couple is the setting aside of a bequest payment. Whether they do so in a lump sum or through periodic payments does not matter.

The motive for establishing a bequest is hard to determine. In order to make the bequest meaningful—more than an idle promise to either their children or themselves—the parents had to either actually set aside or be able to set aside enough wealth to cover the bequest at some future date. The distinguishing feature between targeted and strategic bequests is that the former occurs when the children leave the household, while the latter takes place when the parents reach old age. Obviously, a great deal of time could pass between these two events, and they are not mutually exclusive even between parents and a single child. A farm couple might have given their children a nearby farm or carved one out of their own holdings when the children left home. Many years later they might have promised their remaining land to the child or children who provided care for their parents in old age. At the time the children were born, all the record might show would be the farm couple establishing a bequest fund, either in land or in other assets. One would not be able to determine the ultimate motive or motives. Fortunately, this does not matter, because it is the establishment of the fund that represents the costs of raising children, and not the reason for its being established. In this framework, the specific bequest motive, whether strategic or targeted, is inconsequential. It does not matter what motivates the farmer to make a bequest, it matters only how the cost of the bequest changes with changes in other variables, such as opportunities off the farm or the price of land.

Finally, consider the size of the bequest. If there exists a difference between the size of a targeted bequest and that of a strategic bequest, then the size of the payment into the bequest fund would be different, and this could determine differences in the cost of children. But given the tastes and preferences of a particular family, why should the two be different? The targeted bequest hypothesis explained in chapter 1 states that the size of the bequest must not be less than the amount of wealth the parents possessed when they started adult life. Something close to this figure may be a reasonable empirical approximation. Returning to the hypothetical twin brothers referred to in chapter 1, one living in the Northeast and the other in the Midwest, if they are different only in where they live, then one might expect the bequest fund to differ only by region as well.

For the purpose of calculating the net present value at birth of a child, the value of the bequest payment equals the mean wealth of families just starting out (stage I households; see chapter 3) within the region in which the parents' farm was located. Thus, the present value of the bequest at birth would have been the lump sum needed in 1860 to ensure that the minimum bequest, after compounding, would have been achieved by the time the children left home (assumed to be at age twenty). While the choice of the bequest payment is arbitrary, it nonetheless captures the flavor of the objectives and motives of both altruistic and strategic parents.

The value of children in the provision of old age security came from calculating the present value of an annuity equal to the mean wealth of older parents with no children remaining in the household (stage V households) within each region. Thus, the present value of the potential old age security provided by a child born in 1860 would have equaled the amount of money a farm couple needed to set aside at the birth of their first child in order to secure a farm of average value for elderly couples when they retired or at least when their last child left home. As with the hypothetical bequest fund, the choice of the value of old age security is by necessity somewhat arbitrary, but again, it is consistent with the arguments concerning parents' objectives presented in earlier chapters.

Since the value of future costs and benefits depended on the parents' expectation of the market interest rate, to complete the calculation an interest rate for discounting future costs and benefits is required. Public securities in the North typically yielded between 5 percent and 6 percent during the late antebellum era, but I derived estimates using 3 percent, 6 percent, and 9 percent.[24] Note also that results reported are for an average of males and females, since the decision concerning whether or not to have children had to be made before parents knew the gender of the child. Three sets of estimates have been calculated; one set excludes bequests and old age security, one includes bequests without old age security, and one includes both. Each set of estimates used the three different rates of discount; thus, nine separate estimates of the value of a child at birth have been calculated (table 4.3).

The first set of estimates excludes bequests and old age security. At a 6 percent rate of discount and above, children were net liabilities to their parents in every region (table 4.3). A child represented a net cost of around $50 to his or her parents in the Midwest and on the Frontier, and around four or five times this much in the Northeast. At lower discount rates, midwestern and frontier children became net assets yielding between $50 and $100. A second set of estimates includes the bequest payment but no old age security. As expected, these estimates are lower than the others, and in every case children were net liabilities to their parents, generally costing around $500. When old age security is added, however, the net costs go down considerably, and in a few instances children became net assets. Overall, considering 6 percent as the discount rate closest to market rates during this period,

Table 4.3 Present Discounted Value at Birth of a Child on Northern Farms by Region, 1860

Discount Rate	North	Northeast	Midwest	Frontier
	Without bequests or old age security			
3%	− $96.45	− $188.49	$83.56	$61.30
6%	− 157.11	− 240.97	− 47.80	− 54.34
9%	− 148.86	− 219.31	− 46.21	− 60.55
	With bequests but without old age security			
3%	− 870.33	− 1,324.97	− 690.32	− 505.80
6%	− 592.92	− 880.99	− 483.61	− 373.70
9%	− 398.25	− 585.56	− 295.61	− 243.31
	With bequests and old age security			
3%	276.27	− 157.24	456.29	110.19
6%	− 110.40	− 311.31	1.09	− 73.20
9%	− 158.09	− 302.03	− 55.46	− 93.74

and employing the estimates that either exclude or include both bequests and old age security, the net present value of a child at birth in antebellum northern agriculture was probably between negative $100 and negative $200.

If children represented purely investment goods, then these figures would indicate that on average they were not very financially rewarding investments—a result that should not surprise today's parents. In the South at the same time, the net present value at birth of a slave child was close to zero but positive.[25] Typically, if the net present value of an asset is positive, then a firm will be inclined to purchase more of that asset, and if the net present value is negative, it will purchase less. But in the nineteenth century, as in the twentieth, children provided utility to their parents through the pride and satisfaction parenthood offered, and in the case of free children the utility parents derived from parenthood and the value of children as consumption goods subsidized their value as producers. (Appendix C presents an economic model of farm family fertility illustrating this point.) Thus, one expects the net present value of free children to be less than that of slave children, and it is not surprising that free children on average were not net assets.

How well do these figures correspond with the regional differences in fertility rates discussed in chapter 1? Recall that depending on which measure of fertility is used, birthrates generally rose as one moved westward. Eight out of the nine sets of estimates in table 4.3 show that the value of children in the Northeast was less than that in the Midwest, and that the difference in value exceeded $150. In six of the nine cases in the table, children in the Midwest were more valuable than those on the Frontier; only in the cases including bequests but excluding old age security were frontier children more valuable than those in the Midwest. This result reflects the neo-Malthusian argument that the ease of establishing a farm on the Frontier made bequests there less expensive. Yet in four of the six cases in which midwestern children provided the greatest value to their parents, the difference was less than $50.

What do these results tell us about antebellum fertility rates? Although children turned out to be net costs to their parents in every region of the antebellum North, midwestern and frontier children were more valuable than those in the Northeast. This finding corresponds to the difference betwen northeastern and western fertility rates. The region with the highest crude birthrates, the Frontier, did not have the most valuable children. This distinction goes to the Midwest, though by at least one measure—that of children ever born—the Midwest was the highest fertility region (see table 1.4). Furthermore, fertility rates, the value of children, and agricultural practice in that region all more closely resembled the Frontier than either of those two regions did the Northeast. So those earlier scholars whose explanations of the demographic transition in the antebellum North we reviewed in chapter 1 were correct: Children were more valuable in the least settled regions, but not necessarily because they were much more valuable as producers in that region. In fact teenage males were much more valuable in the Northeast than elsewhere. But the costs of endowing children with either a start in adult life or a bequest in exchange for old age security drove the net cost of a northeastern child higher than in either of the other two regions.

CHAPTER FIVE

Fertility Decline, Economic Growth, and Northern Agriculture

Regardless of region, the northern American farm of 1860 differed considerably from that of 1790. In addition to changes in the operation of the farm, the average farm family had 25 percent fewer children. Still, farms carved from the forests of the Old Northwest and the trans-Mississippi prairies differed from those of the long settled Northeast. Economic change and regional differences in agricultural practice had transformed the roles of women and children and altered the pattern of intergenerational transfers of wealth. Between the founding of the republic and the Civil War such subtle developments had brought about a notable decline in birthrates among rural populations in general and differences in fertility between regions in particular.

Four factors brought about these significant changes in farm family fertility: a westward shift of agricultural production, improvements in transportation, technological change in agriculture that increased labor productivity, and social changes that reduced the farm household's social and economic insularity. Of course, all of these factors affected one another, and causality between external developments and changes that took place within the household ran in both directions. Their net effect on fertility does not always appear clearly. Yet each of these factors had one or more specific characteristics that directly affected fertility decisions in farm families.

Western Migration

By 1860, pioneer families had cleared millions of acres of fertile farmland from the great deciduous forests of the Old Northwest. Beyond these forests, settlers found the rich topsoil of the prairie grasslands. From the Genesee and Susquehanna river valleys in western New York and central Pennsylvania, the western migration and agricultural expansion relocated the frontier a thousand miles west to the plains of Kansas. The contrast between the western prairies and northeastern river valleys altered the nature of frontier settlement and broadened the differences between frontier and settled agriculture. When in 1787 the Northwest Ordinance opened the trans-Appalachian lands to farmers, the main difference between a frontier farm and a settled farm lay in the proportion of time and energy spent on land clearing and farm making. Once settlers had cleared the land, however, farm families on the New York or Pennsylvania frontier in the late eighteenth century practiced agriculture in much the same way as their friends and relatives back East. While one could find differences within the region (the output mix in southeastern Pennsylvania differed from that of the rocky slopes of Vermont), a mixed agriculture of grains, dairy, and livestock products characterized the region as a whole, primarily for on-farm consumption but increasingly for urban and international markets.

The midwestern farmer practiced a different type of agriculture than the northeastern farmer. Frontier farmers in 1860 spent a disproportionate amount of time and energy on land clearing and farm making, just as easterners had done seventy years earlier, but once a farm began to take shape their crop mix and agricultural technique differed from those of easterners. In the production of grains the Midwest early on, and later the Frontier as well, dominated the Northeast by the end of the antebellum era. Geography explained much of the difference. Per acre yields of corn and wheat—the two most important grains by volume—in the newer regions were 50 percent to 100 percent higher than in the older region, and the relatively flat expanses of the Midwest provided more opportunity to profitably employ mechanized implements invented to sow and harvest grains.[1]

The settlement of the Old Northwest and the growth of agricultural production in that region had repercussions for the Northeast. In 1860 the average midwestern and frontier farm produced a marketable surplus of all crops equivalent to 350–400 bushels of corn, which could feed eight or nine men per farm. This average amounted to 50 percent to 100 percent more than the surplus the average northeastern farm produced.[2] Increased competition from midwestern grain caused northeastern farmers to change their crop mix, reducing their production of corn and wheat as a share of their marketable surplus and sending more dairy products, market-garden crops, and hay to market in the growing urban areas of the region.

The western migration had effects on the rural community other than the mix of agricultural products. Differences in the marriage rate accounted for 40 percent of the difference in the total fertility rate between the Northeast and the Midwest and Frontier. Most of the analysis in the previous chapters focused on explaining the other 60 percent—that is, the differences in fertility rates of farm families among the various regions of the antebellum North not accounted for by differences in the incidence of marriage. In an age that took seriously the sanctity of marriage and the family, fertility within marriage dominated total fertility, particulary among rural northern populations; differences in the rate at which people married among the regions thus had a large effect on fertility rates. The relative ease of land acquisition for those who moved west (a requirement for an independent family farm), helped to establish the rural family as an economic unit early in the life cycle of couples in less settled regions. This earlier start in the Midwest and on the Frontier meant the average farm woman there was likely to have more children than did her northeastern counterpart. Also, the great physical hardships pioneers faced induced a disproportionate number of single men to migrate, while women more often arrived at the Frontier already married. So the mix of people that migrated westward had an effect on birthrates as well. The mortality of premodern women during childbirth affected the gender ratio as well. Although by today's standards little health care existed in any region, the complete absence of care on isolated prairie or backwoods farms put women there at greater risk than in the Northeast.

The westward expansion of midwestern agriculture throughout the antebellum era concurrent with the improvement of the transportation network had a number of important effects on the economic value of children in the northern United States. As a result of this expansion, changes in the nature of northeastern agriculture and the differences between the Northeast and Midwest explain part of the regional differences in fertility rates. Opportunities for increasing one's wealth through farm making in the newer regions and the comparative advantage in the production of field crops farmers enjoyed in those regions contributed to fertility differences, both directly and indirectly through competition that induced northeastern farmers to specialize in other products. Frontier opportunities induced out-migration from the Northeast, and those most likely to migrate were people in their most productive years: old enough to begin and maintain a family and farm in the wilderness, yet young enough to expect to live to enjoy the long run returns from such an endeavor. At the same time, population density and urbanization drove up agricultural land values in much of the Northeast. Together, out-migration and higher prices for farmland meant that endowing or bequeathing children a nearby farm became more difficult in the Northeast than on the Frontier; the net cost of children therefore rose in the Northeast, after adjustment for the increased probability that children would not be around to provide support when their parents reached old age. These effects, the result of the targeted and strategic bequest motives discussed in chapter 1, influenced northeastern parents to have fewer children than their midwestern or frontier counterparts. Although changes in northeastern agricultural practice made those teenage boys who remained more productive than those in the Midwest or on the Frontier, the increase in value did not completely offset certain higher costs: the higher probability of lost old age security and the increased expense of bequests.

Transportation

To the south and west, the Ohio and Mississippi rivers defined the boundaries of the Old Northwest. Their tributaries, such as the Miami, Wabash, and Illinois rivers, served as smaller arteries of early trade. Throughout the antebellum era towns and cities sprang up and grew along the banks of these rivers and the shores of the Great Lakes, which served as the region's northern boundary. These cities became the market centers for the sale, storage, processing, and shipping of agricultural products, which were sent down the Mississippi to New Orleans and by sea to the rest of the world. Buffalo, Pittsburgh, Cincinnati, St. Louis, and Chicago all grew and prospered with the lake and river trade.

But lakes stood and rivers ran where nature, not people, decided, and it was not until the late 1820s and 1830s that canals were dug in an attempt to circumvent the often circuitous network of natural waterways. Canals came and went in a few decades. Except for the Erie, few turned out to be profitable for their investors, although, as with any true public good, their social value was greater than their private value. In many cases canals changed the flow of goods. The Erie Canal redirected many northeastern products, formerly shipped to Boston, down the Hudson River to New York City. Similarly, once canals were built along the waterways of the Midwest, trade flowed upriver to the Great Lakes, to Lake Erie in particular, and from there to the Erie Canal and on to New York rather than down the Mississippi to New Orleans, as had formerly been the case.

Canals threatened many established communities along lake and river routes; likewise railroads influenced the flow of goods and doomed many river and canal towns while contributing to the prosperity of others. Railroads connected countless farms and hamlets with outlets for their products. Typically, these connections extended from a town on a minor river to one on a larger river or on one of the Great Lakes, linking the hinterlands in between to world markets. The experience of Indiana illustrates a typical pattern. Early in the century, before canals or railroads, goods loaded around Indianapolis on the westfork of the White River went downriver by flatboat to the Wabash south of Vincennes and on to the Ohio. Later, after completion of the Wabash and Erie Canal, goods went down the canal south of Terre Haute and from there on to Evansville and the Ohio, or they now went in the opposite direction, north to Lake Erie via Fort Wayne. In 1847 a rail line was established between Indianapolis on the White River and the old trading city of Madison on the Ohio. While farmers located in the Wabash basin continued to ship along the Wabash and Erie Canal in the early 1850s, those around Indianapolis and many farmers along both forks of the White as well as the Big and Little Blue rivers now had access to rail. In 1854 the New Albany and Salem Railroad connected the Ohio with Lake Michigan (the famous Monon Line); these and connecting lines had ended much of the trade along the Wabash by 1860.[3]

Economic displacement accompanies technological change just as economic growth does. The Luddites may have reserved for themselves a place in history by their violent response to the former, but the rewards from the latter have been too great to hold back technological innovation. Like the canals, railroads displaced the economic life of some people, while contributing to that of others, all the while facilitating the economic and geographic expansion of the nation. Farmers produced until the cost to them of additional production, including transportation costs, just equaled the expected return. A canal or railroad gave farmers in an ever widening geographical area the opportunity to dispose profitably of their produce. Improved access to markets had two effects, one economic, the other social.

Better transportation meant that northeastern farmers faced increasing competition from western agricultural production. Unless they could cut costs, they would be unable to compete successfully. Yet lower transportation costs also provided northeastern farmers with their clearest advantage over western producers: proximity to the eastern seaboard. Since these costs continued falling faster in the newer regions than in the Northeast, this advantage could not be expected to last indefinitely, but during the late antebellum era certain agricultural products could still be profitably produced on northeastern farms. Improved transportation meant the quicker delivery of larger quantities of crops to market; at the same time the higher population density in general and growth of urban areas in particular throughout the Northeast increased the demand for many products that still could not be competitively shipped from the Midwest and Frontier. Thus, the system of agriculture changed in the Northeast. The average northeastern farm now produced dairy products, particularly fluid milk; market-garden and orchard products; hay; and poultry in greater quantities than the average farm elsewhere.

Before the western migrations, Yankee farmers typically provided self-sufficiency for their families and produced goods, such as wool, maple syrup, potash, lumber, and market-garden crops, for both home use and the market. Many of these farms also grew a small surplus of corn, wheat, buckwheat, or barley to go along with the specialty items for home consumption and sale. The products from the Old Northwest and beyond, mainly corn and other cereals but also livestock, undercut much of the northeastern production of these commodities. While the midwestern farm family typically derived 30 percent of its gross revenue from corn and cereals, the northeastern family received half that percentage from those products. On the other hand, northeasterners received half their total revenue from truck-farm products, compared to 30 percent for midwesterners.

In terms of the value of children these changes had conflicting effects. On the one hand, the shift away from land clearing and later grain farming in the Northeast provided opportunities to profitably increase the production of goods that children were reported to have been particularly adept at, thus increasing their value in that region. Although many contemporary commentators claimed that women and children specialized in certain tasks on the farm, little statistical evidence indicates that within a particular region farms with children produced a different output mix, than those without children. Indeed, within each region farms overwhelmingly produced the same output mix, regardless of household composition or the scale of the farm operation. On the other hand, these changes in the regional pattern of agricultural production induced children to migrate upon reaching adulthood, becoming either farmers in the West or urban workers, thus reducing their value to parents in the Northeast. Taken together, these changes helped lower the value of northeastern children relative to those in the Midwest and on the Frontier.

Mechanization

In addition to the expansion of agriculture into the new lands and the development of a transportation network that made farming there profitable, the technology of farming also changed. Mechanization in agriculture, based on innovative ideas and prototypes constructed by visionaries and eccentrics decades earlier, developed rapidly, and the adoption of horse-drawn implements was well under way in many stages of agricultural production by the end of the antebellum era. Grain drills, reapers, mowers, and threshers all represented old ideas and in some cases old designs, but the antebellum era saw the practical application of the principles behind them and the widespread, though by no means universal, adoption of the machines.

The productivity of agricultural labor in the nineteenth century could be increased by farming on more productive land (western migration); by changing the technology of production by applying fertilizers, rotating crops, and so forth (scientific agriculture); and by using machines where possible (mechanization). Of these, mechanization contributed more to increase output per worker on northern farms (at least in the production of grains) than did either of the other two.[4] How much of the wheat crop was completely or even partially mechanized? The answer will probably never be known, but it is known that farmers employed more than 100,000 reapers and mowers in 1860 and thousands of drills and threshers as well. Since the machines could be jointly rented or owned, in all probability 150,000–200,000 farmers employed horse-powered machines to sow, reap, or thresh their crop. Although this would include less than one-sixth of all northern farms in 1860, the mechanized farms represented the largest and certainly the most progressive agricultural households. If a farm family did not employ machines, it was either because they could not afford the initial capital outlay (unlikely, since credit terms were available), or because they farmed an insufficient acreage of mechanized crops to profitably amortize the investment (more likely, since less than 10 percent of northern farmers sowed enough wheat or hay to break the threshold of 60 or more acres required to profitably employ a reaper or mower).[5]

Mechanization represented perhaps the most tangible form of agricultural progress, but other aspects of farming evolved during the era as well. Selective breeding of livestock, for example, had been well established in Great Britain and parts of continental Europe since the eighteenth century. Farmers of the early republic ignored it to a large extent. By 1860, however, local breeders had become well known, and the process was conducted on farms throughout the North, most commonly in the more settled regions. Similarly, crop rotation, inclusion of fodder crops in the rotation, and use of fertilizers all represented advances that enhanced the productivity of labor. Along with mechanization, they all had potentially conflicting effects on the value of children and thus on fertility rates.

The effects of mechanization often ran in opposite directions, just as with western migration and improvements in transportation. Most obviously, the introduction of labor-saving machines reduced the number of workers needed to cultivate a given area, and at the same time mechanization increased the productivity of those workers who remained. Thus, the adoption of machinery meant a farm couple needed fewer children to help operate a farm of a fixed size, but those children they did have became more valuable. The opportunity to expand the farm by employing farm implements meant a possible increase in the scale of the farm and family size. An increase in scale may have occurred on many midwestern and frontier farms, where the larger farms and greater production of wheat provided more opportunity to employ the implements then available, leading to more children and higher birthrates in those regions.

At the same time that mechanization made farm labor more productive, it may also have permitted a substitution toward less physically strong labor, specifically children. The sowing of wheat required specific human capital, according to narrative evidence, and the harvesting of wheat with a scythe was among the most physically demanding of farm tasks. The mechanical sower, the grain drill, and the reaper replaced these skills with different ones that required their own specific human capital, but allowed workers with less strength and stamina to compete more favorably with fieldhands, making children relatively more valuable. Thus, mechanization paradoxically made children more productive (valuable), yet less essential.

Social Change or "Externalization"

Many of the changes that took place within the farm family, in agricultural practice, and in the pattern of migration were part of a broader social change that has been called "modernization." The problem with employing the word *modernization* in this context is that scholars typically associate modernity with measures such as the extent of urbanization and industrialization. Although urbanization and industrialization caused part of the social change that affected fertility decline in Europe, the early onset of fertility decline in U.S. agricultural communities relative to those of Europe has led historians and demographers to discount modernization as a cause of the pattern of fertility behavior in the United States. No, modernization does not describe the process at work in America.

What is needed instead is a term that describes the turning outward of the farm family beyond the household and the local community toward the world beyond. The term would have to represent children leaving the farm to migrate westward or to a city to work for a merchant or manufacturer; describe a wife realizing she had market opportunities away from the farm as well as on it; describe the selling of an increasing proportion of the output from one's labor to strangers hundreds of miles away; capture the increasing tendency to acquire knowledge and technology from others who more often than not were strangers; and represent a family investing savings in a bank account, equities, or annuities rather than in more farmland to bequeath to children. The best name for this process is *externalization*—the growing interaction, collectively and individually, between the members of the farm household and a widening network of social and economic institutions and participants. This process differs from that of modernization as that term is typically used, because neither industrialization nor urbanization were necessary in order for the process I am describing to occur, though both probably facilitated it.

The interaction of northern yeomen with the wider world and its effects on the course of economic development have not gone unnoticed by scholars.[6] This interaction can be pictured as a series of concentric circles with the farm at the center. First comes the village, town, or county seat. Although American farmers did not actually share output as their European forebears and countless agricultural societies had done, they nevertheless belonged to a wider community. They gathered in town to worship God, celebrate the memorials of a common heritage, display and market goods, and rule one another.

101

The next circle contained the region and nation. Midwestern farmers sent their goods first by flatboat and later by steam down the Mississippi and its tributaries to New Orleans. Canals and railroads connected them with northeastern markets. Finally, there was the international market. The colonial economy had been founded on the Atlantic trade, and for decades progressive American farmers had imported improved breeds of hogs, sheep, and cattle from Europe. The process of externalization involved the increasing replacement of features of the inner circles with those from farther out. The farm family became part of the village; the villagers became midwesterners and then northerners; and they all became Americans. This process manifested itself in numerous ways.

Perhaps nowhere did externalization show itself more clearly than in the changing economic and social roles of children. School attendance increased until, by the end of the era, the overwhelming majority of farm children attended school for some time during the year. There was little difference in attendance among regions, and attendance had been growing in all regions over time. Upon reaching adulthood, children increasingly left their parents' farms and joined the western migration or sold their labor in the market rather than becoming yeomen as their parents had done. The increasing propensity to attend school and migrate to other geographical regions and sectors of the economy meant that children became more costly to raise, and it simultaneously decreased the probability that children would supply old age security for their parents.

Women also experienced a change in their roles. For decades, young women had left their parents' household to work in the New England textile mills. This work experience outside the household set a precedent for later generations of women. Opportunities away from the farm, particularly for young women who once away from the farm may never have returned to an agricultural household, meant an increase in the opportunity cost of any time spent working in the home, including time spent caring for children.

Women who had already married and who remained in a farm household were not directly affected by the experiences of the mill workers, but the evolution of women's roles in society showed up on the farm in other respects as well. Women had once worked in the fields alongside the men. Technological change in the harvesting of wheat and the growth of demand for other products led women to specialize in work around the household. The woman of the house became almost exclusively responsible for the cooking, cleaning, laundering, dairying, and butter and cheese production, and she usually saw to the care of the vegetable garden as well. Changes that increased the value of the mother's time within the household affected the value of children in much the same way as the existence of opportunities off the farm. Although a woman was generally expected to care for her children while doing her household chores, any time spent away from milking and churning; spinning; making sugar, sausage, or preserves; or performing one of a hundred other tasks cost the family real income, just as foregoing outside employment does now.

The increase in productivity brought about through mechanization and western expansion freed farmers and their families to spend time reading and corresponding through agricultural journals. Some antebellum agricultural journals even had a "Ladies Department," and these sections often had women editors. They provided a forum for women and kept them informed about issues such as health, education, and off-farm employment. They did not shy away from the promotion of feminist causes, including the publication of letters promoting women's suffrage.[7] In addition, the spread and growth of county fairs and state and county agricultural societies, many of which presented monetary awards for superior products, promoted the reciprocal flow of information between the farmstead and the rest of society. The picture of the rural hayseed separated from modern life was the creation of an industrial society in which urban boosters viewed those who remained in agriculture as less progressive than themselves. Yet the typical antebellum northern farmer owned more wealth, was more likely to be literate, and maintained a higher standard of living by most measures than the average American or European. Farm families saved money and placed it in savings banks or reinvested it in land, livestock, and equipment. They read newspapers as well as the Bible. Through the growth of the market and other forms of externalization, they increasingly became an integrated part of a broader community, and this meant a greater reliance on one's own wealth for old age security than on the care supplied by children.

Externalization, together with the other factors discussed here, contributed to changes over time and to regional differences in the economic value of children. "The simple extension of settlement kept markets in a continual ferment, and yeast was added by technical changes."[8] Farm couples knew how to control their fertility, and they knew whether it was in their best economic interests to have more children. By the end of the era, children were probably a net cost to their parents in every region. The net cost at birth of an antebellum farm child ranged from around $300 in the Northeast to less than $100 in the Midwest and on the Frontier. It is not surprising that children were a net cost, because they provided utility to their parents as consumption goods as well as farm production and old age security as investment goods. These regional differences in the value of children corresponded roughly, though not always perfectly, with the regional differences in birthrates. The net cost of children reached its highest level in the Northeast. As one might expect, farm couples in this region had the lowest birthrates. The fertility behavior of midwestern and frontier families was similar, and the value of children was closer in those regions as well. So broadly speaking, the value of children did correspond to East-West differences in fertility rates. When we more carefully define the West, however, dividing it into the Midwest and the Frontier, birthrates in these two regions correspond to differences in the value of children, depending on what measure of fertility one chooses, though arguably both lie within some reasonable range of one another.

Research on economic explanations of nineteenth-century fertility rates for farm families has emphasized three aspects of the value of children as causal factors: opportunities to employ children in agricultural production, the costs of bequeathing children a (nearby) farm, and the costs absorbed when children defaulted on the implicit contract to provide their parents with old age security. Migration, transportation, mechanization, and externalization affected each of these potential factors in the long run decline of and regional differences in fertility rates; thus, each of those changes played a role in fertility behavior. To what extent a particular change affected a particular household we cannot say. This study has combined all of these effects and explicitly calculated directly comparable regional estimates of the value of children in farm families at the end of the antebellum era.

Children were net costs to their parents in every region. As producers only, however, the value of young children and teenage girls was greatest in the Midwest, while teenage boys provided the greatest value in the Northeast. Bequests played an important role in calculating the net value of a child, but I have argued that the type of bequest, targeted or strategic, displayed less importance than had been emphasized in earlier work. Indeed most parents probably employed both types of transfers at one time or another, and the decision to grant either one or the other played a larger role in the value of children than which form of the bequest was to be granted. When bequests and

104

old age security were included in the calculation of the value of children at birth, children had their lowest costs in the Midwest, followed closely by the Frontier. The region of lowest fertility, the Northeast, had by far the most costly children.

Perhaps the debate over the regional pattern of rural fertility in the antebellum United States henceforth will focus explicitly on the value of children. Future contributions should explain how they improve the estimates of the value of children reported in this volume. Better estimates of child productivity could possibly be obtained. Estimates of the value of children for earlier (and later) decades would be valuable. Finally, a complete history of the value of children and their roles as both production and consumption goods in the United States and other developed countries could help explain the pattern of fertility over time and in many contemporary developing regions.

The Estimation of Gross Farm Revenue

Although the approach taken in this book emphasizes geographical regions as the appropriate way in which farms should be grouped, as opposed to grouping by political units such as states, the availability of some data exclusively by state dictates using them as economic regions in those cases. Agricultural prices represent such a case. Table A.1 shows the price per unit by state for each of the products either recorded in the census of agriculture or estimated below. Farm-gate prices could not be obtained for every product for every state. In cases in which a state price could not be found, the price in a contiguous state was employed.

As noted in chapter 2, the Eighth Census of Agriculture did not include fluid milk, poultry, eggs, or lumber products. To obtain an estimate of the total amount of milk produced on each farm, first multiply the average milk produced per milk cow by the number of milk cows on each farm. Table A.2 lists the average output of fluid milk per milk cow by state. To obtain the residual fluid milk production after accounting for butter and cheese production, subtract the quantity of milk needed to produce the quantities of butter and cheese reported in the census. (On average it took 10 pounds of fluid milk to make 1 pound of cheese, and 22 pounds to produce 1 pound of butter.) The remainder is the residual fluid milk. The object here is to estimate gross revenue, but this technique underestimates the gross output of dairies and creameries that purchased fluid milk as an input for their operations. To adjust for this fact, farms that had at least one milk cow but a negative quantity of fluid milk following this procedure had

Table A.1 Crop Prices by State, 1859–60 (dollars per unit)

	Wheat (bu)	Rye (bu)	Corn (bu)	Oats (bu)	Rice (lb)	Tobacco (lb)	Cotton (bale)	Wool (lb)	Peas & Beans (lb)	Irish Potatoes (bu)	Sweet Potatoes (bu)	Barley (bu)	Buckwheat (bu)	Wine (gal)	Butter (lb)	Cheese (lb)	Hay (ton)
Northeast																	
Connecticut	1.51	0.87	0.90	0.43	2.49	0.12	44.00	0.37	1.03	0.48	0.51	0.66	0.60	0.26	0.15	0.11	10.30
Maryland	1.22	0.71	0.74	0.38	2.49	0.04	56.00	0.24	0.86	0.73	0.51	0.66	0.40	0.26	0.23	0.11	14.55
New Hampshire	0.98	0.95	0.93	0.45	2.49	0.08	44.00	0.31	1.03	0.48	0.51	0.66	0.59	0.26	0.15	0.11	10.30
New Jersey	1.30	0.84	0.77	0.40	2.49	0.08	56.00	0.51	1.03	0.48	0.51	0.90	0.62	0.26	0.15	0.11	10.30
New York	1.25	0.80	0.68	0.36	2.49	0.08	56.00	0.23	0.86	0.39	0.51	0.65	0.40	0.26	0.17	0.11	13.93
Pennsylvania	1.13	0.69	0.65	0.39	2.49	0.10	56.00	0.13	1.03	0.48	0.51	0.66	0.50	0.26	0.15	0.11	10.30
Vermont	0.98	0.95	0.98	0.43	2.49	0.25	44.00	0.49	1.03	0.48	0.51	0.66	0.59	0.26	0.15	0.11	10.30
Midwest																	
Illinois	0.90	0.40	0.43	0.40	3.98	0.09	56.00	0.32	1.21	0.50	0.51	0.57	0.50	0.26	0.15	0.15	5.68
Indiana	1.00	0.37	0.30	0.33	3.98	0.09	56.00	0.28	1.21	0.48	0.51	0.77	0.45	0.26	0.19	0.11	10.30
Iowa	0.68	0.50	0.30	0.25	3.98	0.09	56.00	0.35	1.21	0.48	0.51	0.44	0.51	0.37	0.19	0.11	10.30
Kansas	0.79	0.48	0.35	0.26	3.98	0.09	56.00	0.33	1.21	0.48	0.51	0.66	0.50	0.37	0.19	0.11	10.30
Michigan	0.89	0.48	0.30	0.26	3.98	0.09	56.00	0.33	1.21	0.48	0.51	0.66	0.59	0.26	0.19	0.11	10.30
Minnesota	0.75	0.41	0.38	0.26	3.98	0.09	56.00	0.33	1.21	0.48	0.51	0.50	0.46	0.25	0.19	0.11	10.30
Missouri	0.89	0.42	0.41	0.33	3.98	0.09	56.00	0.30	1.21	0.48	0.51	0.60	0.47	0.26	0.18	0.11	10.30
Ohio	1.15	0.50	0.50	0.43	3.98	0.09	56.00	0.41	1.21	0.48	0.51	0.55	0.68	0.26	0.13	0.11	10.30
Wisconsin	0.88	0.25	0.41	0.29	3.98	0.09	56.00	0.20	0.87	0.46	0.51	0.69	0.45	0.25	0.13	0.09	5.86

	Clover Seed (bu)	Grass Seed (bu)	Hops (lb)	Hemp (ton)	Flax (lb)	Flax-seed (bu)	Silk (lb)	Maple Sugar (lb)	Molasses (gal)	Beeswax (lb)	Honey (lb)	Cane Sugar (lb)	Poultry (lb)	Eggs (doz)	Fluid Milk (lb)	Lumber (cords)
Northeast																
Connecticut	4.94	2.83	0.15	150.00	0.20	1.61	11.94	0.09	0.90	0.36	0.15	0.07	0.08	0.15	0.07	2.46
Maryland	4.94	2.83	0.18	100.00	0.26	1.61	11.94	0.09	0.90	0.36	0.15	0.07	0.08	0.15	0.07	2.66
New Hampshire	4.94	2.83	0.18	150.00	0.20	1.61	11.94	0.09	0.90	0.36	0.15	0.07	0.08	0.15	0.07	2.34
New Jersey	4.94	2.83	0.13	141.30	0.20	1.50	11.94	0.09	0.90	0.36	0.15	0.07	0.08	0.15	0.07	2.66
New York	5.13	3.06	0.25	141.30	0.20	1.61	11.94	0.09	0.90	0.36	0.15	0.07	0.08	0.15	0.07	2.60
Pennsylvania	4.94	2.83	0.18	141.30	0.26	1.61	11.94	0.09	0.63	0.36	0.15	0.07	0.08	0.15	0.07	1.01
Vermont	4.94	2.83	0.20	150.00	0.16	1.61	11.94	0.09	0.90	0.36	0.15	0.07	0.08	0.15	0.07	3.30
Midwest																
Illinois	4.94	2.83	0.20	100.00	0.20	1.03	11.94	0.08	0.50	0.26	0.15	0.08	0.05	0.08	0.07	2.34
Indiana	4.94	2.83	0.15	100.00	0.20	1.03	11.94	0.08	0.50	0.26	0.15	0.08	0.04	0.08	0.07	1.38
Iowa	4.94	2.83	0.20	100.00	0.20	1.03	11.94	0.08	0.50	0.26	0.15	0.08	0.05	0.08	0.07	1.10
Kansas	4.94	2.83	0.33	100.00	0.20	1.03	11.94	0.08	0.50	0.26	0.15	0.08	0.05	0.08	0.07	2.30 ·
Michigan	4.94	2.83	0.20	100.00	0.20	1.03	11.94	0.08	0.50	0.26	0.15	0.08	0.04	0.08	0.07	1.69
Minnesota	4.94	2.83	0.19	100.00	0.20	1.03	11.94	0.08	0.50	0.26	0.15	0.08	0.06	0.10	0.07	1.44
Missouri	4.94	2.83	0.20	100.00	0.20	1.03	11.94	0.08	0.50	0.26	0.15	0.08	0.05	0.08	0.07	2.34
Ohio	4.94	2.83	0.16	150.00	0.20	1.03	11.94	0.08	0.50	0.26	0.15	0.08	0.04	0.08	0.07	1.09
Wisconsin	6.13	1.95	0.19	100.00	0.20	1.06	11.94	0.08	0.50	0.26	0.15	0.08	0.06	0.10	0.07	1.48

Source: Jeremy Atack and Fred Bateman, *To Their Own Soil: Agriculture in the Antebellum North* (Ames: Iowa State University Press, 1987), tables 13.1–13.5.

109

Table A.2   Poultry, Egg, Fluid Milk, and Lumber Production by State, 1859–60

	Poultry Stock per Improved Acre	Dozens of Eggs per Unit of Poultry	Fluid Milk per Cow (000s of lbs)	Lumber per Unimproved Acre (cords)
Northeastern states				
Connecticut	0.528	8.042	4.203	0.351
Maryland	0.317	3.737	1.906	0.278
New Hampshire	0.192	6.633	3.719	0.316
New Jersey	0.830	4.625	3.510	0.254
New York	0.359	4.661	4.511	0.895
Pennsylvania	0.534	4.457	3.312	0.317
Vermont	0.148	6.184	4.498	0.402
Weighted mean	0.389	4.810	4.125	0.496
Midwestern states				
Illinois	0.423	3.322	1.901	0.303
Indiana	0.439	4.212	1.987	0.456
Iowa	0.450	4.129	2.149	0.314
Kansas	0.372	3.991	2.752[a]	0.015
Michigan	0.525	5.064	3.230	0.779
Minnesota	0.317	3.447	2.752[a]	0.152
Missouri	0.563	2.621	1.480	0.234
Ohio	0.588	3.677	3.315	0.678
Wisconsin	0.319	3.674	2.541	0.178
Weighted mean	0.448	3.826	2.752	0.381
Overall weighted mean	0.428	4.126	2.585	0.424

Sources: Author's calculations from Census Office, Tenth Census, *Report Upon the Statistics of Agriculture Compiled from Returns Received at the Tenth Census* (Washington, D.C.: Government Printing Office, 1883); and Fred Bateman, "Improvement in American Dairy Farming, 1850–1910: A Quantitative Analysis," *Journal of Economic History* 28 (June 1968): 255–73.
[a]Estimate unavailable, regional average employed.

their fluid milk output set at zero. This adjustment increases the gross output of fluid milk (and thus all dairy products) in general and on northeastern farms in particular, and it accounts for the differences between the estimates in table 2.2 and those reported elsewhere.[1]

The tenth census (1880) included counts of the poultry population for the first time. To obtain farm-level estimates of poultry for 1860, the units of poultry per improved acre for 1880 were estimated for the counties from which the farms in the Bateman-Foust sample were drawn. (Table A.2 lists the average poultry production by state.) The product of the county-level ratios of poultry per improved acre for 1880 and the improved acres per farm in 1860 yields an estimate of the number of poultry for a given farm in 1860. Assuming each unit of poultry yielded 4 pounds of meat, multiplying the pounds per farm by the price of poultry per pound from table A.1 gives the estimated dollar value of poultry production for each farm.[2] Note that by using the weight of chickens, which were smaller than other poultry, such as turkeys, these estimates are biased downward. Similarly by omitting game, the consumption of which according to contemporary accounts must have been enormous, total poultry production has been further biased downward.

The 1880 census also included a count of the dozens of eggs produced per household. The ratio of egg output to units of poultry in 1880 yields the dozens of eggs per unit of poultry for the counties from which the townships in the Bateman-Foust sample were drawn. To estimate the dozens of eggs produced on a given farm, multiply the units of poultry per improved acre by the eggs per unit of poultry (shown by state in table A.2); then multiply the resulting figure by the improved acres for each farm. The product of the dozens of eggs per farm and the price per dozen from table A.1 yields the dollar value of eggs produced by a given household in 1860. The estimates of egg production in table A.2 also differ from the 2.16 dozen eggs per chicken reported elsewhere.[3] This figure is on average about half as large as my estimate of dozens of eggs per unit of *all* poultry. Since the number in the denominator of this ratio includes all poultry and not just chickens, a downward bias is already incorporated. Since the 1880 data were collected in the same way as those for 1860 and are chronologically nearer to them than the estimates used to derive the 2.16 figure, I believe that the estimates of poultry and egg production reported here represent the best current estimates for 1860.

To obtain an estimate of the cords of lumber produced on a particular farm in 1860, the cords of wood per unimproved acre, as reported in the 1880 census at the county level were multiplied by the unimproved acres on that farm (table A.2 shows the per acre averages by state). Multiplying the resulting number by the price per cord from table A.1 yields the value of lumber produced per household.

The census also omitted any measure of the returns to wealth. These include the implicit rental value of the farmhouse, the returns from clearing land, any capital gains from land, and the appreciation in the value of livestock. To estimate the implicit rental rate of the farmhouse and structures, one must know the proportion of farm value in structures as opposed to land, livestock, and implements; however, the censuses contain no information on the relative value of different components of the farm until 1910, and the value of the farmhouse was not separated from other structures until 1930. To determine the share of total farm value in structures in 1860, first compare the share of the total value of the farm accounted for by structures from 1910 through 1940. If an upward trend in the relative share of structures can be found, then use the estimate for structures in 1910. If no upward trend appears, then use an average value for the two earliest periods, 1910 and 1920. Ten percent of this figure times total farm value in 1860 yields estimates of the implicit rents due to the household from farm structures. (Table A.3, column 4, lists the average percentage of farm value in structures by state.)

Using recently estimated values for improved acres, the increase in the value of an acre from improving it, v, can be calculated as the difference between the price of an improved acre, p_i, less the price of an unimproved acre p_u.

$$v = p_i - p_u \qquad (A.1)$$

The total value of all the land on a given farm, V, is equal to the sum of the product of p_i and improved acres, I, and p_u, and unimproved acres, U.

$$V = p_i I + p_u U \qquad (A.2)$$

The published censuses contain the value of land and number of improved and unimproved acres, and p_u can be derived as a residual from equation A.2. To directly estimate the share of the increase in the value of land attributable to its improvement, calculate the change in the value of land between any period t and $t + n$.

$$
\begin{aligned}
dV &= V_{t+n} - V_t \\
&= dp_i I + p_i dI + dp_u U + p_u dU + dp_i dI + dp_u dU
\end{aligned}
\qquad (A.3)
$$

The righthand side of equation A.3 contains the components of the difference in the value of land between two periods. The terms with dI represent changes in the value of land due (partly, in the case of the interaction term $dp_i dI$, and entirely, in the case of the term $p_i dI$) to changes in improved acres. Dividing both sides of equation A.3 by

112

Table A.3 Average Annual Rates of Growth in Value of Farms, Land,
and Livestock by State, 1850–60

	Farms, Including Structures	Farms, Land Only	Livestock	Percentage of Farm Value in Structures
Northeastern states				
Connecticut	1.07%	1.80%	3.00%	31%
Maryland	3.62	4.80	4.70	45
New Hampshire	1.90	1.50	1.70	25
New Jersey	2.59	3.30	2.70	44
New York	2.27	3.00	2.00	36
Pennsylvania	2.65	3.60	3.20	57
Vermont	3.39	3.70	1.90	56
Weighted mean	2.76	unavailable	unavailable	unavailable
Midwestern states				
Illinois	8.16	9.40	4.70	15
Indiana	6.22	7.40	2.90	18
Iowa	5.55	6.90	3.90	17
Kansas	N.A.	10.70	4.30	12
Michigan	5.27	6.80	4.90	36
Minnesota	3.95	6.10	5.60	16
Missouri	7.61	6.00	4.70	9
Ohio	4.13	5.20	3.90	23
Wisconsin	2.92	5.60	0.60	24
Weighted mean	6.31	unavailable	unavailable	unavailable
Overall weighted mean	5.02	unavailable	unavailable	unavailable

Sources: Census Office, Seventh Census, *Statistical View of the United States* (Washington, D.C.: A.O.P. Nicholson, 1854); Census Office, Eighth Census, *Agriculture in the United States in 1860* (Washington, D.C.: Government Printing Office, 1864); and Census Office, Fifteenth Census, *Agriculture—Volume II, Part 1—The Northern States* (Washington, D.C.: Government Printing Office, 1932).

dV yields the proportion of the change in the value of land between any two periods due to each source. For example, the share of the total increase in the value of land coming either entirely or partly from improved acres is $(p_i dI + dp_i dI)/dV$. The product of this term and the average annual increase in the value of land per year yields the average increase per farm in farm value due to improved acres. Similar calculations yield the returns from increases in land prices, a pure capital gain. The average annual rates of growth of farm value (including structures), land only, and livestock from this technique are shown by state in table A.3.

Another measure of farm output is the *marketable surplus*—that is, the quantity of output a farm could have disposed of in the marketplace after all on-farm consumption had been accounted for. The estimation of the marketable surplus consists of two steps. First, output must be converted to a *numéraire*. In other words, some standardized measure of physical production must be constructed. Farm production converted to "corn equivalent" bushels based on the net energy factors of each crop represents total physical output. The conversion factors for the major crops relative to wheat are as follows.[4]

Output (Unit)	Conversion Rate	Output (Unit)	Conversion Rate
Wheat (bu)	1.00	Barley (bu)	0.88
Rye (bu)	0.88	Buckwheat (bu)	0.76
Corn (bu)	1.00	Butter (gal)	0.25
Oats (bu)	0.86	Cheese (gal)	0.25
Peas & beans (bu)	0.92	Fluid milk (1,000 lb)	2.00
Irish potatoes (bu)	0.88	Hay (ton)	16.64
Sweet potatoes (bu)	0.95	Meat (lb)	0.10

Clearly, this list is not exhaustive, but the production of such goods as home manufactures, maple sugar, and hemp are difficult to convert to equivalent units of corn. Furthermore, the crops reported here made up the greatest portion of the value of farm output.

The second step consists of subtracting from gross output the consumption of corn equivalent bushels needed for livestock production, seed for the next planting, and household members. Consumption rates by type of livestock recorded in the census are as follows.[5]

Livestock Consumption	Bushels of Corn	Tons of Hay
Horses	12.50	0.75
Mules	8.50	0.51
Milk cows (per 1,000 lbs of milk)	1.00	0.06
Oxen	8.50	0.51
Other cattle	1.50	0.09
Sheep	0.25	0.02
Swine	5.00	0.30

Draft animals received the largest share of feed. Other types of livestock often foraged most of the year. Grasses and hay proved particularly important to eastern farmers located near towns and cities. Although little quantitative evidence exists concerning the amount of hay fed to livestock, by narrative accounts it must have been relatively large. I have assumed that at least half of the net energy of supplemental feeding of livestock came from hay. In addition to the portion of the crop consumed by livestock, it was necessary to set a certain portion aside for the next planting season. Seed requirements are reported by the percentage of the current crop necessary for the same crop mix the next season.[6]

With respect to consumption by household members, a diet for a typical man is more easily constructed than a diet for individual age and gender groups, though many studies of household consumption first estimate the average daily caloric intake of individuals by age and sometimes sex or type of occupation, then calculate the ratio of each age group's consumption to that of men. The caloric intake estimates are often done by direct observation, budget studies, or allocation functions. These functions take measured household output and allocate it among family members according to the minimum physiological requirements by age and perhaps gender. The results of several such studies listed in the bibliographical essay have been adjusted for the age distribution of northern farm families and were used to construct a "medium" set of consumption estimates. These estimates are as follows. A man in one year consumed 771 pounds of milk through assorted dairy products, 200 pounds of meat, 8.0 bushels of corn, 1.6 bushels of wheat, and 3.5 bushels of other crops and legumes.[7] The corn equivalents among the other crops have been allocated according to their relative weights in the output of the average northern farm and the relative energy value as described above. The relative weights of output in a region were used to determine the relative quantities consumed. In other words, if corn composed 25 percent of the energy output in a county, then I assumed it composed 25 percent of the consumption on the farms in that county. The man's diet described here equals 41.4 corn equivalent bushels.

Table A.4 presents the results of the estimation of the net crop surplus for northern farms. The average surpluses range from a high of 435 bushels of corn on midwestern farms, to a low of 299 bushels on northeastern farms. In other words, the average midwestern farm could feed roughly eleven additional men or the equivalent of their average annual consumption, and in the Northeast the average farm could feed roughly seven additional men. The relationship found earlier between gross revenue and type of ownership ceases to hold when output is measured by the potential marketable surplus in bushels of

Table A.4 Average Net Crop Surplus by Region and Type of Ownership, 1860
(measured in corn equivalent bushels)

Region	Owner-Operator	Part-Owner	Tenant	Regional Mean
Northeast	291	320	383	299
Midwest	424	464	499	435
Frontier	339	391	296	338
North	363	405	431	372

Sources: See tables 2.1–2.3, appendix A, and text.

corn rather than dollars. In the Northeast and Midwest tenants produced a larger surplus than owners or part-owners. The explanation for this lies in differences in the output mix of the two types of farms: tenants were more likely to specialize in grains, and grains provided more energy per unit of output. Furthermore, tenants had little incentive not to overcrop their land, ignoring crop rotation and fertilizer; thus, their larger surplus in grains may reflect the incentive structure of being a tenant. Landlords could account for this in the rents they charged tenants, but this would show up in net revenue and not physical output (see chapter 4). Whether northern farms were owner- or tenant-operated, they generated a sizable marketable surplus by 1860. The interaction with local, regional, and international markets that these surpluses entailed had effects on the economics of the farm household, including fertility decisions.

Chi-Square Test Results from Comparing Output Mix Between Regions

To test the hypothesis that the output mix between any two types of farms, whether within the same region at different life cycle stages or among different regions but at the same life cycle stage, we must test to see if the proportion of revenue coming from each of the five categories of output was the same for each type of farm. To test whether or not the differences in the output mix among regions and life cycle stage are statistically significant, we can use the chi-square test. If s_{ij} is the share of income coming from output category $i = 1, 2, \ldots, 5$ for region or household type $j = 1, 2$, then the null hypothesis can be written as

$$H_o: s_{11} = s_{12}, s_{21} = s_{22}, \ldots, s_{51} = s_{52}$$

In other words, the null hypothesis says that the proportion of total revenue coming from a particular category on two different types of farms was the same for each category. The comparison of the output shares follows a chi-square distribution with four $(i - 1)$ degrees of freedom. At the 5 percent level of significance the chi-square value against which the null hypothesis must be tested is 9.96, and 7.78 at the 10 percent level.

Table B.1 Chi-Square Test Results from Comparing Crop Portfolios by Life Cycle Stage and Region

	Owners					Tenants				
	I	II	III	IV	V	I	II	III	IV	V
Results from comparing the same stage among different regions										
Northeast & Midwest	14.91[a]	14.71[a]	13.04[a]	17.10[a]	15.37[a]	9.61[b]	9.10[b]	10.47[a]	17.31[a]	11.73[a]
Northeast & Frontier	9.50[a]	8.10[a]	7.79[b]	10.10[a]	10.16[a]	4.26	1.09	5.71	N.O.	N.O.
Midwest & Frontier	2.72	1.93	1.50	1.23	3.46	6.40	5.89	4.47	N.O.	N.O.
Results from comparing different stages within same region										
Northeast										
I	—					—				
II	0.14	—				0.26	—			
III	0.26	0.18	—			0.28	0.16	—		
IV	0.50	0.25	0.68	—		2.37	3.04	2.78	—	
V	0.42	0.26	0.60	0.71	—	1.81	2.61	1.77	5.03	—
Midwest										
I	—					—				
II	0.34	—				1.17	—			
III	0.17	0.05	—			1.54	0.37	—		
IV	0.31	0.30	0.16	—		1.99	1.14	0.08	—	
V	0.59	0.48	0.28	0.05	—	1.26	5.98	5.27	6.19	—
Frontier										
I	—					—				
II	0.54	—				0.93	—			
III	0.88	0.13	—			1.12	2.97	—		
IV	0.52	0.17	0.34	—		N.O.	N.O.	N.O.	—	
V	4.68	3.25	3.35	3.05	—	N.O.	N.O.	N.O.	N.O.	—

[a] The probability of obtaining a test statistic this large when the null hypothesis is true is less than 0.05.
[b] The probability of obtaining a test statistic this large when the null hypothesis is true is less than 0.10.

Table B.2 Chi-Square Test Results from Comparing Crop Portfolios by Farm Size (Acres) and Region

	Owners					Tenants				
	0–40	41–80	81–120	121–60	161+	0–40	41–80	81–120	121–60	161+
	Results from comparing the same farm size among different regions									
Northeast & Midwest	10.19ᵃ	11.68ᵃ	14.22ᵃ	18.35ᵃ	17.43ᵃ	12.32ᵃ	13.44ᵃ	21.71ᵃ	6.25	8.51ᵇ
Northeast & Frontier	3.55	7.78ᵇ	10.03ᵃ	12.64ᵃ	11.18ᵃ	14.86ᵃ	4.45	17.30ᵃ	1.20	9.83ᵇ
Midwest & Frontier	3.61	3.29	1.25	1.18	0.97	5.38	3.64	4.58	11.00ᵃ	8.89ᵇ
	Results from comparing different farm sizes within the same region									
Northeast										
0–40	—					—				
41–80	0.40	—				1.39	—			
81–120	0.52	0.07	—			2.47	0.29	—		
121–160	0.53	0.22	0.11	—		5.57	2.31	1.23	—	
161+	1.72	0.96	0.63	0.36	—	13.68ᵃ	8.11ᵇ	6.32	5.06	—
Midwest										
0–40	—					—				
41–80	1.51	—				3.80	—			
81–120	2.58	0.33	—			19.43ᵃ	11.25ᵃ	—		
121–160	4.86	1.32	0.40	—		7.42	2.36	4.69	—	
161+	6.64	2.33	0.98	0.21	—	11.06ᵃ	4.53	2.56	0.85	—
Frontier										
0–40	—					—				
41–80	2.48	—				3.56	—			
81–120	4.01	0.95	—			23.40ᵃ	16.08ᵃ	—		
121–160	6.17	3.02	0.69	—		7.76	2.35	19.54ᵃ	—	
161+	6.57	3.25	0.72	0.12	—	4.69	1.61	15.92ᵃ	2.26	—

ᵃThe probability of obtaining a test statistic this large when the null hypothesis is true is less than 0.05.
ᵇThe probability of obtaining a test statistic this large when the null hypothesis is true is less than 0.10.

119

Appendix B

Two different sets of tests were conducted. The first set compares the distributions of output within and among the various regions by life cycle stage. The second set compares the distributions of output within and among the various regions by farm size. Tables B.1 and B.2 contain the results from the first and second sets of tests, respectively.

120

APPENDIX C

An Economic Model of Farm Family Fertility

The standard neoclassical approach to the theory of the consumer postulates that consumers maximize a utility function, with goods and services as arguments, subject to an income constraint. Similarly, firms maximize profits or minimize costs subject to a production constraint. The theory of the allocation of time extends the utility maximization approach by viewing the household as a producer of basic commodities, such as sleep, health, entertainment, and other goods. Market goods and time make up the inputs for the production of these basic commodities, and consumers maximize utility from the consumption of these basic commodities subject to a full income constraint.[1] Farm family fertility, or more specifically the demand for children, can be incorporated into this framework with two important additions. First, bequests must be explicitly accounted for; second, farm households must be recognized as producers (profit maximizers) as well as consumers (utility maximizers).

This dual role of the farm household still holds today. However, due to increases in agricultural productivity and the rise of industrialism, the size of the agricultural labor force and the number of farm households have declined both absolutely and relative to their non-agricultural counterparts. Today, individuals predominantly sell their labor to firms, and economists now focus on the allocation of labor between market work and leisure. Analysis of contemporary questions concerning the household revolves around individuals as consumers of goods or sellers of labor. To take such an approach in trying to explain household behavior in nineteenth-century farm households would most likely yield misleading results since most did not sell their labor in the market but rather worked on family-owned and -operated farms.

Although numerous neoclassical models of fertility behavior have been developed, they typically omit a key variable in the relationship between parent and child and thus in fertility decisions, namely, a bequest motive or the role of intergenerational transfers of wealth. These models typically explain the decline of farm birthrates over time, emphasizing changes in the opportunity cost of a farm woman's time as the main explanatory variable. Chapter 1 showed that in 1860 the regions of the North displayed little difference in the employment of married women off the farm. Therefore, these models must be modified to address questions concerning the change in nineteenth-century child-bearing.

Consider first the farm household as a consumer. Assume that all consumption decisions are made jointly by the husband and wife. The discounted flow of services from children is

$$C = \sum_{t=0}^{T} [1/(1 + r)^t] \, c_t \qquad (C.1)$$

where c_t is the quantity of (nonproductive) services parents receive from children in any given period t, including the joy and satisfaction of raising children; r is the rate at which future services are discounted; and T is the number of periods between the present and the death of the husband and wife.[2] The discounted flow of services from other goods is expressed by

$$X = \sum_{t=0}^{T} [1/(1 + r)^t] \, x_t \qquad (C.2)$$

where x_t is the continuous flow of services from other goods. The parents derive utility or satisfaction from the consumption of the services from children and all other goods. The utility function for the household would thus be given by

$$U = U(C, X) \qquad (C.3)$$

Since the household produces child services and other goods, it follows that c_t and x_t must be produced in each period from the inputs of market goods, goods produced on the farm, and time. For example, the production of child services included any storebought goods, such as cooking utensils, shoes, or toys; goods produced on the farm, such as clothes or food; and the parent's time in supervising children. The production functions of these products are given by

$$c_t = f_c (y_{tc}, T_{tc})$$
$$x_t = f_x (y_{tx}, T_{tx})$$

$$(C.4)$$

where y_{tc}, y_{tx} are collections of inputs of goods produced on the farm and purchased in the market that go into the production of c_t and x_t, respectively. T_{tc} and T_{tx} are vectors of time inputs in producing c_t and x_t. In addition, the inputs can be expressed by the production relationships

$$T_{tc} = t_c c_t \qquad T_{tx} = t_x x_t$$
$$y_{tc} = b_c c_t \quad \text{and} \quad y_{tx} = b_x x_t$$

$$(C.5)$$

where t_c and t_x are vectors of time per unit of c_t and x_t, respectively, and b_c and b_x are vectors of market goods and home goods per unit of c_t and x_t.

Assume that the opportunity cost of the husband's or wife's time in producing a household good is the wage rate available off the farm, w. Together with equation C.5 this assumption implies that the full prices—that is, the price including the opportunity cost of time—of child services and other goods are

$$p_c^* = b_c p_c + w t_c$$
$$p_c^* = b_x p_x + w t_x$$

$$(C.6)$$

where p_c and p_x are vectors of market prices of household-produced and market goods that go into the production of child services and other goods respectively.

Let C^* be the household's initial stock of children. The proportion of C^* living on the farm in period t is given by

$$\theta_t = \theta (m_t, w)$$

$$(C.7)$$

where m_t is the child mortality rate, and w represents a measure of opportunities off the farm, for example, the wage in nearby urban areas or the returns from farming inexpensive land on the frontier. Assuming that there were no significant regional differences in the mortality of children, the flow of child services at time t is a decreasing function of opportunities away from the farm for children.[3]

$$c_t = \theta\,(w)C^* \tag{C.8}$$

Equation C.8 indicates that at any point in time the product of the initial stock of children and the proportion of children remaining on the farm or within the farm community yields the flow of child services.

Since how much the farm family consumes is determined by how much the farm produces, the farm household as a producer must be specified. Children contributed to the productive process on the family farm. The productive services from the stock of desired children are expressed as

$$q_t = a_t\,\theta_t\,C^* \tag{C.9}$$

where a_t is the periodic rate of flow of productive services from children. The profit function for the farm would be expressed as

$$\pi_t = pf(q_t,\,H_t,\,T_{ft},\,K_t) - w(H_t + T_{ft}) - rK_t \tag{C.10}$$

where the variables are as follows:

p = vector of prices of farm output
$f(\ )$ = vector of output of products
H_t = hired labor
T_{ft} = adult household labor
K_t = capital and land
$w,\,r$ = prices of inputs of labor and capital respectively.

The husband and wife's time constraint is expressed as the sum of their respective constraints

$$T_t = T_t^H + T_t^W \tag{C.11}$$

where both the husband's and wife's time is divided into time spent on the production of child services, the production of other goods, or market production. These can be further divided into time spent on the consumption of child services, c, the consumption of other goods and services, x, and farm labor, f, or

$$T_t^H = T_{ct}^H + T_{xt}^H + T_{ft}^H$$
$$T_t^W = T_{ct}^W + T_{xt}^W + T_{ft}^W \qquad \text{(C.12)}$$

So the sum of the husband's and wife's time spent in consumption is

$$T^* = (T_t^H - T_{ft}^H) + (T_t^W - T_{ft}^W) = T_t - T_{ft} \qquad \text{(C.13)}$$

The quantity of farm labor hired other than those laborers living in the farm household was relatively small; therefore, hired labor other than that recorded in the household is ignored, and the labor input from all household sources is given as $L_t = H_t + T_{ft}$.

From the discussion of bequests in chapter 4, within a given region one can think of the bequest payment as an annuity with periodic payments, B, times the number of children in the household, $\theta_t C^*$. So in any given period the bequest payment is

$$b_t = B\theta_t C^* \qquad \text{(C.14)}$$

Keep in mind that all one observes is that parents set aside this payment. It could be used as a targeted bequest; it might be a retirement account; or it might be a strategic bequest payment reflecting the fear that children would abandon parents in their old age. The important point is that it does not matter why parents set aside this periodic payment. It only matters that they do so.

In any given period, t, the resources available to the family must equal the expenditures and other obligations or claims on those resources. As noted in chapter 2 the resources of the family include wealth and the revenues from operating the farm, less the costs of doing so. The result of this is net profit, π_t, in equation C.10. Adding to net profit the returns to the family's wealth, rW_t, and subtracting the costs in both time and goods of children and other goods, $b_c p_c c_t$ and $b_x p_x x_t$ respectively, and the bequest payment, b_t, yields the single period resource constraint:

$$\pi_t + rW_t - b_c p_c c_t - b_x p_x x_t - b_t = 0 \qquad \text{(C.15)}$$

The time constraint of equation C.11 and the resource constraint of equation C.15 can be combined to yield the intertemporal (or lifetime-planning horizon), full wealth constraint of the farm family.

$$Y = \sum_{t=0}^{T} 1/(1 + r)^t [rW_t + wT_t^* + pf(a_t\theta_t C^*, L_t, K_t)$$
$$- rK_t - wL_t - p_c^* \theta_t C^* - p_x^* x_t - B\theta_t C^*] = 0 \tag{C.16}$$

Equation C.16 represents the fact that the lifetime expenditures on farm inputs, children, consumption, and bequests must equal lifetime income from wealth, labor, and the operation of the farm. The farm family's problem is to maximize utility from the consumption of goods and services from children, equation C.3, subject to this constraint. For convenience of exposition, let $i = 1/(1 + r)^t$. Together with the full wealth constraint, the first-order conditions are

$$U_C * \sum_{t=0}^{T} i\theta_t + \Gamma \left[\sum_{t=0}^{T} i(pa_t\theta_t f_c - p_c^* \theta_t - \theta_t B) \right] = 0 \tag{C.17}$$

$$U_x - \Gamma \sum_{t=0}^{T} ip_x^* = 0 \tag{C.18}$$

$$\mu pf_L - w = 0 \tag{C.19}$$

$$\mu pf_K - r = 0 \tag{C.20}$$

where equations C.17 and C.18 represent the marginal utility conditions, and C.19 and C.20 are the familiar results that the value of the marginal product of each input equals its wage. Note that changes in f_L and f_K over time are ignored, and $\mu = \sum_{t=0}^{T} i$.

If the functional forms of U and f were known, then one could solve the system of four equations in four unknowns. The choice variables are the number of children, C, the quantity of other consumption goods, X, the farm labor input, L, and the capital input, K. But in real life we rarely know the utility and production functions; therefore, only a few comparative statics results can be obtained. To see these, first rewrite equation C.17 as follows:

$$\left[U_C * \sum_{t=0}^{T} i\theta_t \right] \Big/ \Gamma = \left[\sum_{t=0}^{T} i(p_c^* \theta_t + \theta_t B - pa_t\theta_t f_c) \right] > 0 \tag{C.21}$$

Equation C.21 demonstrates the important result that when children enter the utility function of parents, parents attach a premium to rearing children, which causes their value as producers to be less than their cost. In other words, the value of the utility services provided by children subsidizes their productive services. This result indicates that even if children contribute a great deal to farm production, they may still have positive net costs, excluding their value as consumption goods, and it explains why the net present value of a child is negative in table 4.3.

Another interesting result occurs from combining and rearranging equations C.17 and C.18. This yields the familiar condition that the ratio of the marginal utilities equals the ratio of the full prices. In other words, at current prices parents get as much satisfaction per dollar spent on children as they do on other goods.

$$\left[U_c * \sum_{t=0}^{T} i\theta_t\right] \Big/ U_X = \Gamma\left[\sum_{t=0}^{T} i(p_c^* \theta_t + \theta_t B - pa_t\theta_t f_c)\right] \Big/ \sum_{t=0}^{T} ip_x^* \quad \text{(C.22)}$$

Equation C.22 shows the importance of calculating the value of children as producers, explicitly accounting for bequests, and considering the opportunity costs of a mother's time in fertility decisions. The greater the productivity of a child, the higher the fertility rate, all other things being equal. Similarly, if the periodic bequest payment rises or the opportunity cost of a mother's time increases, then to keep the equality of the price ratio and the marginal rate of substitution, fewer children will be demanded. Assuming that the marginal utility of children is positive, $U_C > 0$, but diminishes as more children are born, $U_{CC} < 0$, one should note from equation C.22 the law of demand at work. If a decrease in the full price of a child occurs, for example, through an increase in the marginal productivity of children (f_c) or a decrease in the bequest payment (B), then the marginal utility of children relative to other goods and services will be too high to maintain the equality. Since the marginal utility of children is diminishing, the consumption of more child services—that is, an increase in the number of children—is called for. On the other hand, if there is an increase in the price of children, for example, an increase in the price of goods or time spent in raising them (p_c^*) or in the bequest payment (B), then the marginal utility of children will be too low relative to the marginal utility of other goods and services. The consumption of fewer child services—that is, a decrease in the number of children—will follow.

At this point readers should recall from chapter 1 how some scholars—in fact, the majority of those studying these issues—have argued that children were more valuable in the less settled regions because of both increased work opportunities and lower costs of bequests. Equation C.22 points out the importance of separating all of the components that go into estimating the value of children. To see this, consider farms in two different regions. The value of children in production may be greater in one region than in the other, but the parent's contribution to the bequest fund may be greater in that region as well, thus offsetting the advantage in production.

The predictions concerning fertility behavior from this model consist of the net effect that a change in opportunities off the farm has on the demand for the initial stock of children within a region, and the differences in the effect between regions. Opportunities off the farm affect productivity, parents' time, and bequests. The sign and magnitude of the derivative, dC/dw, illustrate the net result of these separate effects. Obtaining this derivative is not trivial, however.

The bordered hessian matrix is derived by totally differentiating the first-order conditions with respect to the choice variables C^*, X, L, K, and the constraint Γ.

$$
\left[\sum_{t=0}^{T} I(pa_t \theta_t f_c - p_c^* \theta_t - B\theta_t) \right] dC^* - \left[\sum_{t=0}^{T} Ip_x^* \right] dX
$$
$$
+ [pf_L - w]dL + [pf_K - r]dK = -dY
\tag{C.23}
$$

$$
\left[U_{cc} \sum_{t=0}^{T} I\theta_t + \Gamma \left[\sum_{t=0}^{T} (pa_t \theta_t f_{cc}) \right] \right] dC^* + \left[U_{cx} \sum_{t=0}^{T} I\theta_t \right] dX
$$

$$
+ \left[\Gamma \sum_{t=0}^{T} (pa_t \theta_t f_{ck}) \right] dK + \Gamma \left[\sum_{t=0}^{T} (pa_t \theta_t f_{cL}) \right] dL
$$

$$
- \left[\sum_{t=0}^{T} I(p_c^* \theta_t + \theta_t B - pa_t \theta_t f_c) \right] d\Gamma = - \left\{ \left(-\Gamma \sum_{t=0}^{T} Ib_c \theta_t \right) dP_c \right.
\tag{C.24}
$$

$$
\left. + \left[U_c \sum_{t=0}^{T} I\theta' + \Gamma \sum_{t=0}^{T} I(pa_t \theta_t f_c - (p_c^* \theta' + t_c \theta_t) - \theta' B) \right] dW \right\}
$$

$$U_{xc}dC^* + U_{xx}dX - \left[\sum_{t=0}^{T} Ip_x^*\right]d\Gamma = -\left[-\Gamma \sum_{t=0}^{T} Ib_x\right]dp_x \quad \text{(C.25)}$$

$$pf_{LC}dC^* + pf_{LL}dL + pf_{LK}dK + [pf_L - w]\Gamma = dw \quad \text{(C.26)}$$

$$pf_{KC}dC^* + pf_{KL}dL + pf_{KK}dK + [pf_K - r]d\Gamma = dr \quad \text{(C.27)}$$

Totally differentiating the first-order conditions allows one to solve for dC^*; however, the cross partial derivatives include so many varying effects that the model would not be very valuable in yielding testable hypotheses without either estimating the signs of the cross partials or making some assumption about them. As noted above, it is difficult to estimate directly the household production functions, and in the absence of any information concerning the signs, I assume that the cross partials are zero.

Let the matrix of second partials be A, and let the matrix of second partials with the ith row replaced be A_i. Then from Cramer's rule the effect of a change in off-farm opportunities on fertility can be determined from

$$dC^*/dw = |A_1|/|A| \quad \text{(C.28)}$$

where, from above, the determinant of A is

$$|A| = U_{cc} \sum_{t=0}^{T} i\theta_t|A_{11}| + \sum_{t=0}^{T} i[(pa_t\theta_t f_c) - (p_c^* + B)\theta]|A_{15}| \quad \text{(C.29)}$$

and the determinant of A_1 is

$$|A_1| = -\sum_{t=0}^{T} i[U_c\theta' + \Gamma(pa_t f_c\theta' \\ - (t_c\theta_t + p_c^*\theta' + B\theta'))]|A_{11}|dw \quad \text{(C.30)}$$

The signs of the determinants determine the sign of dC^*/dw. The first term in $|A|$ is negative by the assumption of diminishing marginal utility; further assuming diminishing marginal productivity, the first-order conditions imply that

$$|A_{15}| = U_{xx} \sum_{t=0}^{T} i(pa_t\theta_t f_c - p_c^*\theta_t - \theta_t B)f_{kk}f_{tt} > 0 \qquad (C.31)$$

Thus, together these two results imply that $|A|$ must be less than zero. With respect to the sign of $|A_{11}|$, writing out the determinant indicates that

$$|A_{11}| = \left(-\sum_{t=0}^{T} ip_x\right)^2 p^2 f_{kk} f_{11} > 0 \qquad (C.32)$$

This result implies that the sign of $|A_1|$ depends upon the sign of

$$a'_{11} = -\sum_{t=0}^{T} i[U_c\theta' + \Gamma(pa_tf_c\theta' - (t_c\theta_t + p_c^*\theta' + B\theta'))] \qquad (C.33)$$

Clearly, dC^*/dw will be less than zero so long as sign of a'_{11} is greater than zero. Equation C.33 can be rewritten as

$$a'_{11} = \sum_{t=0}^{T} i[\theta'\Gamma(b_c p_c + B - pa_t f_c) - Z] \qquad (C.34)$$

where $Z = U_c\theta' - \Gamma t_c\theta_t(1 + \epsilon)$, where $\epsilon < 0$ is the elasticity of θ with respect to w. We know $\theta' < 0$ and $\Gamma > 0$. So it must be that the term in parentheses and Z determines the sign and magnitude of dC^*/dw. Note that the term in parentheses is the negative of the present value of a child at birth. This measure is precisely the one upon which all economic models of fertility ultimately depend. The results in table 4.3 indicate that this measure was probably negative; therefore, for $dC^*/dw < 0$, it must be that $Z < 0$. Z will be negative if either the absolute value of ϵ is less than one or if $|U_c\theta'| > |\Gamma t_c\theta_t(1 + \epsilon)|$. An ϵ less than one would say that the percentage change in the proportion of children leaving the farm was less than the percentage change in the opportunity cost of off-farm activity, w. In other words, suppose the wages of young men in urban manufacturing or on the western frontier increased by 10 percent, then the proportion of children remaining on northeastern farms would decrease by less than 10 percent, certainly a plausible result. Furthermore, the closer to zero ϵ is, the larger in absolute value dC^*/dw. That is, the more responsive fertility is to changes in off-farm opportunities, the smaller the change in fertility required to restore equilibrium after a change in off-farm opportunities.

The results of the model indicate two implications for differences in regional birthrates in the antebellum North. First, not surprisingly, regions in which children were of the greatest net value (lowest net cost) to their parents should have displayed the highest birthrates. The results in chapter 4 illustrate how the antebellum North confirmed this prediction. Second, the region in which the population displayed the greatest response to changes in opportunities off the farm (the region experiencing the most out-migration) should see its fertility at a lower level but declining more slowly than those of regions with an inelastic response to opportunities off the farm. So over time, perhaps several decades or longer, there should be a convergence of regional fertility rates. This is in fact what occurred in the United States.

It is interesting to note that to this point the fertility debate in the social science literature has not revolved around the sign of dC^*/dw. Both the targeted and the strategic bequest hypotheses imply (assume?) that the sign was negative, but they disagree on the cause. I have shown that it is difficult to empirically separate the two arguments, because increases in opportunities off the farm corresponded to increases in population density. Farm families in the long settled rural areas of New England encountered the greatest opportunities in other areas, but New England also had the most densely settled rural areas. To come to grips with these differences, we need to explicitly estimate the present value of a child at birth in each of the regions; this is what I have done in chapter 4.

Notes

Preface and Acknowledgments

1. Fred Bateman and James D. Foust, *Agricultural and Demographic Records of 21,118 Rural Households Selected from the 1860 Manuscript Censuses*, magnetic tape, Indiana University, 1974.

Chapter One
The Decline of Rural Birthrates in the Antebellum North

1. Alexis de Tocqueville, *Democracy in America*, 2 vols. (New York: D. Appleton, 1899), 1:39.

2. Estimates of the distribution of wealth for the United States are drawn from Lee Soltow, *Men and Wealth in the United States, 1850–1870* (New Haven: Yale University Press, 1975), p. 99; and Jeremy Atack and Fred Bateman, *To Their Own Soil: Agriculture in the Antebellum North* (Ames: Iowa State University Press, 1987), p. 88. The comparisons between antebellum Ohio and England and France are from Lee Soltow, "Tocqueville's View of the Northwest in 1835: Ohio a Generation after Settlement," in *Essays on the Economy of the Old Northwest*, ed. David C. Klingaman and Richard K. Vedder (Athens: Ohio University Press, 1987), pp. 139–41. Comparisons of the distribution of wealth among different groups in postcolonial America are from Peter Lindert, *Fertility and Scarcity in America* (Princeton: Princeton University Press, 1978), p. 226. Evidence reported by the Federal Reserve Board shows that during the 1980s the proportion of total wealth owned by the richest 1 percent rose from around 30 percent to over 35 percent.

3. James T. Lemon, *The Best Poor Man's Country: A Geographical Study of Early Southeastern Pennsylvania* (Baltimore: Johns Hopkins University Press, 1972).

4. The complete quotation is: "Of all occupations from which gain is secured, there is none better than agriculture, nothing more productive, nothing sweeter, nothing more worthy of a freeman" (Omnium autem rerum, ex quibus

aliquid acquiritur, nihil est agri cultura melius, nihil uberius, nihil dulcius, nihil homine libero dignius). Marcus Tullius Cicero, *De officiis* (Cambridge: Harvard University Press, 1951), p. 155.

5. Thomas Jefferson, *Writings of Thomas Jefferson*, 20 vols. (Washington, D.C.: Thomas Jefferson Memorial Association, 1904), 19:18.

6. Harriet Martineau, *Society in America* (Garden City, N.Y.: Doubleday, 1962), p. 292.

7. Quoted in Paul W. Gates, *The Farmer's Age: Agriculture 1815–1860* (New York: Holt, Rinehart, and Winston, 1960), p. 86.

8. Quoted in Robert Swierenga, *Pioneers and Profits: Land Speculation on the Iowa Frontier* (Ames: Iowa State University Press, 1968), p. 10.

9. Early birthrates are from Morton O. Schapiro, "Land Availability and Fertility in the United States, 1760–1870," *Journal of Economic History* 42 (September 1982): 594. Biological maximum for noncontracepting Homo sapiens is from Henry Shryock, Jacob Siegel, and Associates, *The Methods and Materials of Demography*, condensed edition, ed. Edward G. Stockwell (Orlando, Fla.: Academic Press, 1976), p. 276.

10. Tocqueville, *Democracy in America*, 2:438.

11. Ezra Seaman, *Essay on the Progress of Nations* (New York: C. W. Benedict, 1843), pp. 364–65; and George Tucker, *Progress of the United States in Population and Wealth in Fifty Years* (1855; New York: Augustus M. Kelly, 1964), pp. 58, 104–5.

12. Strictly speaking, the child-woman ratio reported in table 1.2 is not a birthrate, although it often correlates with measures such as the crude birthrate. The crude birthrate has drawbacks as a measure of fertility, since it too is heavily influenced by the age structure of a population. Since the frontier population was younger than those in more settled regions, one expects higher crude birthrates in frontier communities.

13. Ansley Coale and Melvin Zelnick, *New Estimates of Fertility and Population in the United States* (Princeton: Princeton University Press, 1963), p. 36.

14. Coale and Zelnick, *New Estimates of Fertility and Population in the United States*, p. 35.

15. Wendell Bash, "Differential Fertility in Madison County, New York, 1865," *Millbank Memorial Fund Quarterly* 33 (April 1955): 186; and Bash, "Changing Birth Rates in Developing America: New York State, 1840–75," *Millbank Memorial Fund Quarterly* 41 (April 1963): 163–64.

16. To obtain this measure, first subtract the total number of farm sites available in a region from the number of potential households, proxied by the number of young white males. If the result is positive, then an excess demand for farm sites existed; to obtain a proportion of demanders unsatisfied, divide this figure by the total number of males. If the result is negative, then there was an excess supply of farm sites; to obtain a proportion of surplus sites, divide this figure by the total number of sites. The resulting proportions ranged from −1.00 to +1.00, with +1.00 representing, at least by this measure, complete economic stress.

17. Donald Leet, "Human Fertility and Agricultural Opportunities in Ohio

Counties: From Frontier to Maturity, 1810–1860," in *Essays in Nineteenth Century Economic History: The Old Northwest*, ed. David C. Klingaman and Richard K. Vedder (Athens: Ohio University Press, 1975), pp. 138–58; and Leet, "The Determinants of the Fertility Transition in Antebellum Ohio," *Journal of Economic History* 36 (June 1976): 359–78.

18. Atack and Bateman, *To Their Own Soil*, pp. 58–60.

19. Schapiro, "Land Availability," p. 589.

20. Colin Forster and G. S. L. Tucker, *Economic Opportunity and White American Fertility Ratios: 1800–1860* (New Haven: Yale University Press, 1972), p. 100.

21. The word *theory* is used here in the sense given to it by economists— that is, as part of the optimal choices people make subject to a constraint on their resources.

22. A "synthetic" total fertility rate, the average number of live births a married woman could be expected to have during her life, can be calculated from census data as follows:

$$R = B[((L - F)/S) + 1]$$

where B is the proportion of women who marry, L is the average maternal age at last birth, F is the average maternal age at first birth, and S is the average interval between children.

23. Atack and Bateman, *To Their Own Soil*, p. 63. These figures have been adjusted for the downward bias inherent in this calculation, following the suggestion of Richard Steckel, "Antebellum Southern White Fertility: A Demographic and Economic Analysis," *Journal of Economic History* 40 (June 1980): 335–37.

24. Richard A. Easterlin, "Population Change and Farm Settlement in the Northern United States," *Journal of Economic History* 37(March 1976): 59.

25. Etienne van de Walle and John Knodel, "Europe's Fertility Transition: New Evidence and Lessons for Today's Developing World," *Population Bulletin* 34 (1980): 18; and Ansley J. Coale and Roy Treadway, "A Summary of the Changing Distribution of Overall Fertility, Marital Fertility, and the Proportion Married in the Provinces of Europe," in *Decline of Fertility in Europe*, ed. Ansley J. Coale and Susan Cotts Watkins (Princeton: Princeton University Press, 1986), pp. 31–181.

26. Frank Notestein, "Economic Problems of Population Change," in *Proceedings of the Eighth International Conference of Agricultural Economists, 1953* (London: Oxford University Press, 1953), p. 18.

27. Atack and Bateman, *To Their Own Soil*, p. 46.

28. Alfred Conrad and John Meyer, "The Economics of Slavery in the Antebellum South," *Journal of Political Economy* 66 (April 1958): 95–122; Robert Fogel and Stanley Engerman, *Time on the Cross* (Boston: University Press of America, 1974), pp. 74–77; Eva Mueller, "The Economic Value of Children in Peasant Agriculture," in *Population and Development*, ed. Ronald Ridker (Baltimore: Johns Hopkins University Press, 1976); and Mead Cain, "The Economic Activities of Children in Villages in Bangladesh," *Population Development Review* 3 (1977): 201–27.

29. Michael Haines, "The Use of Model Life Tables to Estimate Mortality for the United States in the Late Nineteenth Century," *Demography* 16 (May 1979): 289–312.

30. Paul David and Warren Sanderson cite a postbellum survey in which only 12.5 percent of the women who responded used no form of positive contraception. Among the most often used techniques were douches, the rhythm method, and condoms. See Paul A. David and Warren C. Sanderson, "Rudimentary Contraceptive Methods and the American Fertility Transition to Marital Fertility Control, 1855–1915," in *Long Term Factors in American Economic Growth*, ed. Robert Gallman and Stanley Engerman (Chicago: University of Chicago Press, 1986), pp. 307–90. For a summary of antebellum contraceptive techniques, see Lee L. Bean, Geraldine P. Mineau, and Douglas Anderton, *Fertility Change on the American Frontier* (Berkeley: University of California Press, 1989), pp. 29–31.

31. Atack and Bateman, *To Their Own Soil*, p. 69, with adjustments following Steckel, "Antebellum Southern White Fertility," pp. 335–37.

32. An excellent summary of this view can be found in John C. Caldwell, *Theory of Fertility Decline* (New York: Academic Press, 1982).

33. Quoted in R. Carlyle Buley, *The Old Northwest*, 2 vols. (Bloomington: Indiana University Press, 1950), 2:329.

34. Richard A. Easterlin, George Alter, and Gretchen A. Condran, "Farms and Farm Families in Old and New Areas: The Northern United States in 1860," in *Family and Population*, ed. Tamara Hareven and Maris Vinovskis (Princeton: Princeton University Press, 1978), pp. 34–35.

35. Ibid.

36. Lee Soltow and Edward Stevens, *The Rise of Literacy and the Common School* (Chicago: University of Chicago Press, 1981), pp. 120–21.

37. Easterlin, "Population Change and Farm Settlement," p. 61.

38. Richard Easterlin, "Does Human Fertility Adjust to the Environment?" *American Economic Review* 61/2 (1971): 401; and Allan G. Bogue, "Comment on 'Population Change and Farm Settlement in the Northern United States'," *Journal of Economic History* 37 (March 1976): 76–81.

39. Easterlin, "Population Change and Farm Settlement," pp. 63–64.

40. William A. Sundstrom and Paul A. David, "Old-Age Security Motives, Labor Markets, and Farm Family Fertility in Antebellum America," *Explorations in Economic History* 25 (April 1988): 164–97.

41. Quoted in Sundstrom and David, "Old-Age Security Motives," p. 177.

42. The term *child default* was first used by Jeffrey G. Williamson in 1986 in an unpublished manuscript, "Fertility Decline, Immigration and Child Default: Evidence from Nineteenth-Century Rural England."

43. Rober Ransom and Richard Sutch, "Did Rising Out Migration Cause Fertility to Decline in Antebellum New England?" Cal-Tech Social Science Working Paper 610, 1986, p. 47.

44. Ransom and Sutch, "Rising Out Migration," p. 14.

45. Marvin McInnis, "Childbearing and Land Availability: Some Evidence from Individual Household Data," in *Population Patterns in the Past*, ed. Ronald D. Lee (New York: Academic Press, 1977), pp. 201–27.

Chapter Two
The Value of Output and the Division of Labor on the Family Farm

1. Harriet Martineau, *Society in America* (abridged ed.; Garden City, N.Y.: Doubleday, 1962), p. 182.

2. James Hall, *Statistics of the West, at the Close of the year 1836* (Cincinnati, 1836), p. 62, quoted in R. Carlyle Buley, *The Old Northwest*, 2 vols. (Bloomington: Indiana University Press, 1950), 1:174.

3. Alexis de Tocqueville, *Democracy in America*, 2 vols. (New York: D. Appleton, 1899), 2:674.

4. *New England Farmer* 8 (1855): 459; also quoted in Clarence Danhof, *Change in Agriculture: The Northern United States, 1820–1860* (Cambridge: Harvard University Press, 1969), p. 136.

5. Thomas Jefferson, *Notes on the State of Virginia* (Chapel Hill: University of North Carolina Press, 1955), p. 85.

6. Martineau, *Society in America*, p. 182.

7. Gregory Clark, "Productivity Growth Without Technical Change in European Agriculture Before 1850," *Journal of Economic History* 47 (June 1987): 419–32.

8. Productivity figures are from Clark, "Productivity Growth," pp. 419–32; John Komlos, "Agricultural Productivity in America and Eastern Europe: A Comment," *Journal of Economic History* 48 (September 1988): 655–64; and Gregory Clark, "Productivity Growth Without Technical Change in European Agriculture: Reply to Komlos," *Journal of Economic History* 49 (December 1989): 979–91.

9. Yield data are from Jeremy Atack and Fred Bateman, *To Their Own Soil: Agriculture in the Antebellum North* (Ames: Iowa State University Press, 1987), pp. 170–74; B. H. Slicher van Bath, *Agrarian History of Western Europe: A.D. 500–1850* (London: Arnold, 1963), pp. 280–82; and Komlos, "Agricultural Productivity," 657.

10. To see this mathematically, let $Q = (Q_1, Q_2, \ldots, Q_N)$ be a collection of quantities of different types of farm output. For example, Q_1 might be bushels of corn, Q_2 bushels of wheat or pounds of butter, and so forth. Let $P = (P_1, P_2, \ldots, P_N)$ be a collection of prices per unit of each of these quantities. The value of crop output will be C.

$$C = P \cdot Q = \sum_{i=1}^{N} P_i Q_i \qquad (2.1)$$

11. Gary Becker, "A Theory of the Allocation of Time," *Economic Journal* 75 (September 1965): 497–99.

12. Let S and H stand for the value of slaughtered livestock and home manufactures and R be the sum of the different types of unearned income. Equation 2.2 gives the full income of the farm household.

$$Y = (P' \cdot Q') + S + H + R \qquad (2.2)$$

P' and Q' now include the prices and quantities of poultry, eggs, fluid milk, and lumber.

13. Clarence Danhof, "Farm-Making Costs and the 'Safety Valve': 1850–1860," *Journal of Political Economy* 49 (June 1941): 343.

14. Leo Rogin, *The Introduction of Farm Machinery* (Berkeley: University of California Press, 1931), p. 197. Much of the material in this section comes from this classic source.

15. J. W. Oliver, *History of American Technology* (New York: Ronald, 1956), pp. 254–56.

16. Rogin, *Introduction of Farm Machinery*, pp. 126–27, 133–34.

17. Atack and Bateman, *To Their Own Soil*, p. 200.

18. Laura Ingalls Wilder, *Farmer Boy* (New York: Harper and Row, 1971), pp. 127–28.

19. Rogin, *Introduction of Farm Machinery*, p. 196.

20. Harriet Martineau, *Society in America*, 3 vols. (London: Saunders and Otley, 1837) 1:329, 2:243.

21. Wilder, *Farmer Boy*, pp. 170–72.

22. *Western Farmer* 1 (1840): 60; also quoted in Percy Bidwell and John Falconer, *History of Agriculture in the Northern United States, 1620–1860* (Washington: Carnegie Institution, 1925), p. 276.

23. William C. Howells, *Recollection of Life in Ohio from 1813 to 1840* (Cincinnati: Robert Clarke, 1895), p. 156; quoted in Bidwell and Falconer, *History of Agriculture*, p. 163.

24. Laura Ingalls Wilder, *Little House in the Big Woods* (New York: Harper and Row, 1971), p. 29.

25. David Hackett Fischer, *Growing Old in America* (New York: Oxford University Press, 1977), p. 228.

26. David Schob, *Hired Hands and Plowboys* (Urbana: University of Illinois Press, 1975), pp. 142, 200–201.

27. *Working Farmer* 13 (1861): 193; also quoted in Danhof, *Change in Agriculture*, pp. 148–49.

28. Schob, *Hired Hands and Plowboys*, pp. 130–49.

29. Wilder, *Farmer Boy*, pp. 279–81.

30. Wilder, *Little House in the Big Woods*, p. 17.

31. Bidwell and Falconer, *History of Agriculture*, p. 128.

32. Ibid., p. 375.

33. Howard Johnson, *A Home in the Woods: Oliver Johnson's Reminiscences of Early Marion County* (Indianapolis: Indiana Historical Society, 1951), p. 164, quoted in Paul Wallace Gates, *The Farmer's Age: Agriculture: 1815–1860* (New York: Holt, Rinehart and Winston, 1960), p. 244.

34. Martin Welker, *Farm Life in Central Ohio Sixty Years Ago* (Cleveland: Western Reserve Historical Society, 1895), p. 50, quoted in Bidwell and Falconer, *History of Agriculture*, p. 163.

35. Schob, *Hired Hands and Plowboys*, p. 200.

36. *New England Farmer* n.s. 8 (May 1856): 206; also quoted in Linda Borish, "Farm Females, Fitness, and the Ideology of Physical Health in Antebellum New England," *Agricultural History* 3 (Summer 1990): 25.

37. Wilder, *Farmer Boy*, p. 198.

38. Gates, *The Farmer's Age*, p. 241.

39. Atack and Bateman, *To Their Own Soil*, p. 154.

40. For technical reasons explained in appendix A, the estimates of the production of dairy products for the Northeast differ from recent estimates of Jeremy Atack and Fred Bateman, "Yankee Farming and Settlement in the Old Northwest," *in Essays on the Economy of the Old Northwest*, ed. David C. Klingaman and Richard K. Vedder (Athens: Ohio University Press, 1987), p. 91.

41. *American Agriculturalist* 21 (1862): 41; also quoted in Gates, *The Farmer's Age*, p. 247.

42. Wilder, *Farmer Boy*, p. 203.

43. Ibid., pp. 164–65.

44. W. R. Smith, *Observations on the Wisconsin Territory* (Philadelphia, 1838), pp. 65–67, quoted in Buley, *The Old Northwest*, 2:137.

45. Paul Wallace Gates, *Landlords and Tenants on the Prairie Frontier* (Ithaca: Cornell University Press, 1973), p. 50.

46. Stanley Lebergott, in *Essays on the Economy of the Old Northwest*, " 'O Pioneers': Land Speculation and the Growth of the Midwest," ed. David C. Klingaman and Richard K. Vedder (Athens: Ohio University Press, 1987), pp. 36–58.

47. Danhof, *Change in Agriculture*, p. 138.

48. Gates, *The Farmer's Age*, p. 56.

49. *American Agriculturalist* 18 (1859): 172.

50. *American Agriculturalist* 19 (1860): 273–74.

51. *Ohio Cultivator* 14 (1858): 22.

52. Gates, *The Farmer's Age*, p. 81.

53. Danhof, *Change in Agriculture*, pp. 104, 138; and Stanley Lebergott, "The Demand for Land: The United States, 1820–1860," *Journal of Economic History* 45 (June 1985): 187–88.

54. Martineau, *Society in America* (abridged ed.), p. 132.

55. Lebergott, " 'O Pioneers' ", p. 51.

56. Estimates are from Martin Primack, "Land Clearing under Nineteenth-Century Techniques: Some Preliminary Calculations," *Journal of Economic History* 22 (December 1962): 484–97; Robert Ankli, "Farm-Making Costs in the 1850s," *Agricultural History* 48 (January 1974): 51–70; and Lebergott, "The Demand for Land," pp. 181–212.

57. Lebergott, "The Demand for Land," p. 189.

58. *Ohio Cultivator* 15 (1859): 2.

59. *Ohio Cultivator* 15 (1859) 118–19.

60. *New England Farmer* 11 (1859): 78–79.

61. *American Agriculturalist* 17 (1858): 259.

62. U.S. Department of Commerce, *Historical Statistics of U.S. from Colonial Times to 1970* (Washington, D.C.: Government Printing Office, 1975), pp. 459–60.

63. Atack and Bateman, *To Their Own Soil*, pp. 132–33. The average cost of clearing land reported by Atack and Bateman could have differed from the marginal cost. The extent to which this occurred depended on the returns to scale in land clearing. No evidence exists for believing they were not constant.

64. Danhof, "Farm-Making Costs," pp. 345–46; and Primack, "Land Clearing," pp. 484–97.

65. This depiction comes from William N. Parker, *Europe, America, and the Wider World, Vol. 2* (Cambridge: Cambridge University Press, 1991), p. 127.

66. Another, more technical reason exists for why the 1850 estimates may be too high. The coefficients from the regressions from which those results came are biased upward. It is not unreasonable to expect that the location of farmland with respect to urban markets and transportation resources contributed to explaining both the value of the land and the degree of settlement. The closer to cities and transportation facilities a farm was located, the more likely it was that it had been established early on, and thus had a higher ratio of improved to unimproved acres and a greater value. It follows that a location variable should be included in any model explaining land values. Atack and Bateman *To Their Own Soil*, pp. 139–40, estimate such a model; as one would expect, they find a location premium in states closer to urban markets. If the correlation between the omitted variable and the included variable is greater than zero, then the expected value of the estimated coefficients is greater than the true value. Thus, the 1850 estimates of the value of converting an acre of land from unimproved to improved status may be biased upward.

67. Comparisons with other estimates come from the following sources. Per capita gross national product (GNP) estimates are from Robert Gallman, "Gross National Product in the United States, 1834–1909," in *Output, Employment, and Productivity in the United States after 1800* (New York: Columbia University Press, 1966), pp. 13–67. Figures for regional per capita income come from Robert Fogel and Stanley Engerman, "The Economics of Slavery," in *The Reinterpretation of American Economic History* (New York: Harper and Row, 1971), p. 335. Farm income figures are from Atack and Bateman, "Yankee Farming and Settlement," p. 91; and Marvin Towne and Wayne Rasmussen, "Farm Gross Product and Gross Investment in the Nineteenth Century," in *Trends in the American Economy in the Nineteenth Century*, ed. William Parker, (Princeton, N.J.: Princeton University Press, 1960), pp. 255–312. Although all these estimates yield different measures of per capita income, in general the relationship of each to those reported in tables 2.1–2.4 is of the expected magnitude.

Chapter Three
The Allocation of Farm Labor and the Life Cycle of the Household

1. Lutz Berkner, "The Stem Family and the Developmental Cycle of the Peasant Household," *American Historical Review* 77 (April 1972): 398–412; Berkner, "The Use and Misuse of Census Data for the Historical Analysis of Family Structure," *The Journal of Interdisciplinary History* 5 (Spring 1975): 721–38; and Berkner, "Household Arithmetic: A Note," *Journal of Family History* 2 (Spring 1977): 159–63.

2. Philip J. Greven, Jr., *Four Generations: Population, Land, and Family in Colonial Andover Massachusetts* (Ithaca: Cornell University Press, 1970).

3. David Hackett Fischer, *Growing Old in America* (New York: Oxford University Press, 1977), p. 56. On the increase of *inter vivos* transfers and the decline of parents' bargaining power, see Carole Haber, *Beyond Sixty-Five: The Dilemma of Old Age in America's Past* (Cambridge: Cambridge University Press, 1983), pp. 15–16. Carole Shammas, Marylynn Salmon, and Michel Dahlin, *Inheritance in America from Colonial Times to the Present* (New Brunswick: Rutgers University Press, 1987), p. 121, report that *inter vivos* transfers made up fewer than 20 percent of all farm transfers in postbellum Iowa.

4. Mean wealth in 1860 is from David Galenson and Clayne Pope, "Economic and Geographic Mobility on the Farming Frontier: Evidence from Appanoose County, Iowa, 1850–1870," *Journal of Economic History* 49 (September 1989): 651.

5. A. V. Chayanov, *The Theory of the Peasant Economy*, ed. Daniel Thorner, Basile Kerblay, and R.E.F. Smith (Homewood, Ill.: Irwin, 1966), p. 134.

6. Ibid., pp. 148–49, 189.

7. Ibid., p. 135.

8. This finding is supported by Jeremy Atack and Fred Bateman, *To Their Own Soil: Agriculture in the Antebellum North* (Ames: Iowa State University Press, 1987), pp. 219–21.

9. See, for example, William N. Parker, "Agriculture," in *American Economic Growth*, ed. Lance Davis et al. (New York: Harper and Row, 1972), p. 370.

10. Economists use this index, known as the Herfindahl index, to measure the concentration of market share among firms within a particular industry. It is calculated as follows.

$$\text{Index} = \sum_{i=1}^{N} [\text{revenue from category } i/\text{total revenue}]^2 \qquad (3.1)$$

For a discussion of its use, see Douglas F. Greer, *Industrial Organization and Public Policy*, 2nd ed. (New York: Macmillan, 1984), p. 101.

11. Although the Herfindahl index yields different measures of concentration when the products are grouped differently or not at all, the general finding of increased specialization in less settled regions conflicts with recent research on this issue by Mary Eschelbach-Gregson; see Gregson, "Specialization and Commercialization in Late Nineteenth-Century Midwestern Agriculture: Missouri as a Test Case," University of Illinois, unpublished mimeo, 1991.

12. The null hypothesis can be written as

$$H_0: s_{11} = s_{12}, \quad s_{21} = s_{22}, \ldots, s_{51} = s_{52}$$

where s_{ij} is the share of income coming from output category $i = 1,2, \ldots, 5$ for region or household type $j = 1,2$.

13. Robert V. Hogg and Allen T. Craig, *Introduction to Mathematical Statistics*, 4th ed. (New York: Macmillan, 1978), p. 74.

14. In passing it should be noted that even when the life cycle stages were altered to include both male and female teenagers in the stage III households, the results obtained from testing differences between average output remained almost identical.

15. Gavin Wright, *Political Economy of the Cotton South: Households, Markets, and Wealth in the Nineteenth Century* (New York: W. W. Norton, 1978), p. 56.

16. Atack and Bateman, *To Their Own Soil*, pp. 126–27.

Chapter Four
The Economic Value of Women and Children in Northern Agriculture

1. Labor force data for the antebellum era are from Eleanor von Ende and Thomas Weiss, "Labor Force Changes in the Old Northwest," in *Essays on the Economy of the Old Northwest*, ed. David C. Klingaman and Richard K. Vedder (Athens: Ohio University Press, 1987), p. 115.

2. Jeremy Atack and Fred Bateman, *To Their Own Soil: Agriculture in the Antebellum North* (Ames: Iowa State University Press, 1987), p. 46.

3. David Schob, *Hired Hands and Plowboys* (Champaign: University of Illinois Press, 1975), especially the chapters titled "Hired Boy" and "Hired Girl."

4. By definition a production function, $f(X, Y)$, where X and Y are inputs, is homogeneous of degree r if $f(tX, tY) = t^r f(X, Y)$. When returns to scale are constant, $r = 1$. If the constant-returns-to-scale assumption is violated, then the absolute value of an input's marginal contribution might be inaccurate. The relative productivity estimates, however, require only homogeneity, not necessarily homogeneity of degree 1. For example, let MP_f be the marginal contribution of farm women and MP_m be the marginal contribution of farm men; homogeneity implies: $MP_f = tf_f$, $MP_m = tf_m$, and $MP_f/MP_m = tf_f/tf_m = f_f/f_m$ and this holds for all r.

5. This relationship, known as Euler's theorem, is shown in equation 4.1:

$$Y = \sum_{i=1}^{N} w_i X_i \qquad (4.1)$$

where w_i is the marginal contribution to farm output of X_i.

6. The value of output going to the household labor inputs, Y^*, can be represented mathematically as in equation 4.2:

$$Y^* = Y = \sum_{j=1}^{n} w_j X_j = \sum_{k=n+1}^{N} w_k X_k \qquad (4.2)$$

The econometric estimation of equation 4.2 would take the following form:

$$Y^* = \alpha + \sum_{k=1}^{K} \beta_k X_k + \epsilon \qquad (4.3)$$

where α is a constant, X_k is the K different types of household labor, and ϵ is

142

a vector of errors. For now, we assume the errors display the Gauss-Markov properties necessary to obtain the best linear unbiased estimates of β from ordinary least squares estimation. These properties include the errors being independent, identically distributed, with a mean of zero, and with a constant and finite variance. The problem with meeting these assumptions is discussed below.

7. This residual or accounting profit shows up in the intercept, α, in equation 4.3. The ratio of profit to the investment in capital, land, and livestock yields the profit rate or rate of return on equity for the farm.

8. The returns to land, explicit rents for tenants, and implicit rents for owners, as well as the share of output going to livestock, feed, and seed are from appendix A. The estimation of the number of hired hands per farm is from Lee A. Craig, "The Value of Household Labor in Antebellum Northern Agriculture," *Journal of Economic History* 51 (March 1991): 73. The wages of hired hands are from Atack and Bateman, *To Their Own Soil*, p. 241, table 13.7. I assume an implicit rate of return to capital of 6 percent.

9. Mead T. Cain, "The Economic Activities of Children in a Village in Bangladesh," *Population and Development Review* 3 (1977): 201–27, describes the experiences of children in developing countries; for slaves in the antebellum South, see Robert W. Fogel and Stanley L. Engerman, *Time on the Cross: The Economics of American Negro Slavery* (Boston: University Press of America, 1984), p. 42; and for the antebellum North, see Schob, *Hired Hands and Plowboys*, p. 173.

10. As the quality of farm management, an omitted variable, increased, there may have been an increase in hired labor, an included variable; thus, the error term in equation 4.3 might be correlated with the independent variables. The farm size dummy corrects for this correlation. Although the problem of multicollinearity may have been introduced by this procedure, since farm size and labor may be correlated, the coefficients will remain unbiased and efficient. A dummy variable was also included for tenant farms, but the coefficient was not significantly different from zero, and when the tenant dummy and size dummies were included together, the former was quite small and not statistically significant.

11. The model to be estimated is

$$Y^* = \alpha + \beta_1 CHILD1 + \beta_2 CHILD2$$

$$+ \beta_3 TEENF + \beta_4 TEENM + \beta_5 ADULTF \qquad (4.4)$$

$$+ \beta_6 ADULTM1 + \beta_7 ADULTM2 + \beta_8 SIZE + \epsilon$$

Due to the presence of heteroskedastic errors, I estimated the model using the generalized least squares estimation technique in order to obtain unbiased and efficient estimates of the coefficients. Equation 4.4 was first estimated by the ordinary least squares method, but the quantities obtained for household labor varied widely, particularly for adult male labor, and showed evidence of heteroskedasticity. Testing for multiplicative heteroskedasticity of the form

$\sigma_k^2 = \sigma^2 \exp(\xi \text{ADULTM1})$, one cannot reject the hypothesis that $\xi \neq 0$. Since the error variance depends on the number of adult males, correcting for heteroskedasticity consists of multiplying the dependent variable and each of the regressors by the inverse of the square root of ADULTM1.

12. The generalized least squares estimation excludes an intercept, so the R^2 values are difficult to interpret and for this reason were not reported.

13. The wage rates are from Atack and Bateman, *To Their Own Soil*, p. 242.

14. Claudia Goldin and Kenneth Sokoloff, "Women, Children and Industrialization in the Early Republic: Evidence from the Manufacturing Censuses," *Journal of Economic History* 42 (December 1982): 741–74; and Goldin and Sokoloff, "The Relative Productivity Hypothesis of Industrialization," *Quarterly Journal of Economics* 99 (August 1984): 461–88.

15. Atack and Bateman, *To Their Own Soil*, p. 261.

16. The profit rates were calculated by multiplying the proportion of farms greater than eighty acres times the coefficient on the dummy variable, adding the result to the profit coefficient, and then dividing the sum by the average value of the farms in each region. The profit rate for the frontier farms calculated by this method is 14.7 percent, but Atack and Bateman, *To Their Own Soil*, p. 261, have no equivalent estimate for comparison.

17. Atack and Bateman, *To Their Own Soil*, p. 288, find a similar relationship between profitability and farm size.

18. The inclusion of the farmer's labor on the righthand side of equation 4.4 may bias the estimates of adult males, since there may be some correlation between the farmer and excluded variables, such as the weather and the quality of land within and between farms. Since the profit coefficient includes returns to the farmer beyond his opportunity wage as a laborer, one wants to measure the marginal contribution of a prime-age adult male with the ADULTM1 variable. To test the sensitivity of the results in table 4.2 to the definitions of this variable, I subtracted from gross revenue the average wage of a hired hand in each state in the sample and one adult male between the ages of nineteen and fifty-four from the ADULTM1 variable. There was no significant change in any of the labor variables. Only the PROFIT coefficient was larger, reflecting the difference between the farmer's contribution as a laborer and his contribution as manager and owner. These results show that the model captures the intended effect in the original regression.

19. These results were obtained by purging the contributions of children in land clearing from the estimates of their total contribution. I did this by subtracting from full household income the component due to increases in the value of farmland due to improving acreage from the lefthand side of equation 4.4. To the extent that the value of land varied with improved acres, and improved acres varied with the labor input, labor's contribution will be captured by the coefficients in equation 4.4. The proportion of the returns to land attributable to labor can be proxied by the proportion of the increase in the value of land due to improving acreage, as estimated in chapter 2. The intercept reflects the proportion not attributable to labor.

20. For adults the relative rankings remain the same, but as expected there is a larger effect on the coefficients in the Midwest than elsewhere.

21. It is possible that the low coefficient for northeastern teenage girls is due to their living in one household and working in another. If they were working in other households as domestics, then the fundamental conclusion that teenage girls specialized in household production would not be changed. If they did agricultural work on another farm, then the model understates their contribution to market production. Teenage girls, however, seldom hired out to perform agricultural labor other than possibly tending to the milking on northeastern farms (see chapter 2 above).

22. Recall that dairy products composed the majority of the value of the additional products not listed in the census (see chapter 2 above).

23. Richard Steckel, "The Health and Mortality of Women and Children, 1850–60," *Journal of Economic History* 48 (June 1988): 333–34; and Ansley J. Coal and Paul Demeny, *Regional Model Life Tables and Stable Populations*, 2nd ed. (New York: Academic Press, 1983), p. 45.

24. Sidney Homer and Richard Sylla, *A History of Interest Rates*, 3rd ed. (New Brunswick: Rutgers University Press, 1991), pp. 304–5.

25. Fogel and Engerman, *Time on the Cross*, p. 76.

Chapter Five
Fertility Decline, Economic Growth, and Northern Agriculture

1. Jeremy Atack and Fred Bateman, *To Their Own Soil: Agriculture in the Antebellum North* (Ames: Iowa State University Press, 1987), p. 172.

2. See appendix A, and Atack and Bateman, *To Their Own Soil*, p. 221.

3. James H. Madison, *The Indiana Way: A State History* (Bloomington: Indiana University Press, 1986), pp. 75–78, 153–58.

4. William N. Parker and Judith V. Klein, "Productivity Growth in Grain Production in the United States, 1840–60 and 1900–10," in *Output, Employment, and Productivity in the United States after 1800* (Princeton: Princeton University Press, 1966), pp. 523–82.

5. Atack and Bateman, *To Their Own Soil*, p. 199.

6. William N. Parker, *Europe, America, and the Wider World: Vol. 2, America and the Wider World* (Cambridge: Cambridge University Press, 1991).

7. Frances W. Kaye, "The Ladies Department of the *Ohio Cultivator*, 1845–1855: A Feminist Forum," *Agricultural History* 50 (April 1976): 414–23.

8. Parker, *Europe, America, and the Wider World: Vol. 2*, p. 141.

Appendix A
The Estimation of Gross Farm Revenue

1. Jeremy Atack and Fred Bateman, "Yankee Farming and Settlement in the Old Northwest," in *Essays on the Economy of the Old Northwest*, ed. David C. Klingaman and Richard K. Vedder (Athens: Ohio University Press, 1987), p. 91.

2. Estimates of the average weight per unit of poultry are from Jeremy Atack and Fred Bateman, *To Their Own Soil* (Ames: Iowa State University Press, 1987), p. 231.

3. Ibid., p. 231.

4. F. B. Morrison, *Feeds and Feeding* (Ithaca: Morrison, 1955), table II; and United Nations Food and Agricultural Organization, *Technical Conversion Factors for Agricultural Commodities* (Rome: Food and Agriculture Organization, 1962), pp. 315–31.

5. These estimates are recorded in bushels of corn and derived from U.S. Patent Office reports from the 1850s.

6. Seed requirements are from Atack and Bateman, *To Their Own Soil*, p. 214.

7. Atack and Bateman, *To Their Own Soil*, chap. 12, use 771 pounds of milk, 200 pounds of meat, and 13.5 bushels of corn equivalents.

Appendix C
An Economic Model of Farm Family Fertility

1. Gary Becker, "A Theory of the Allocation of Time," *Economic Journal* 75 (September 1965): 493–517.

2. For simplicity assume that the husband and wife die at the same time. Although this assumption is not realistic, it implies that the planning horizon for the joint decisions made by the husband and wife is only valid as long as they both are alive.

3. The measure of child quality in period t can be expressed as $\Phi_t = \Phi(y_{tc}, T_{cc})$. Since there is little reason to expect quality to differ among regions, assume that the quality index is the same in all regions, letting Φ equal unity. This assumption stems from the question posed in chapter 1 concerning the twin brothers identical in every way except that they live in two different regions.

Bibliographical Essay

Chapter 1
The Decline of Rural Birthrates in the Antebellum North

For comments from contemporary travelers on economic, political, and social equality in antebellum America relative to Europe, see Alexis de Tocqueville, *Democracy in America*, 2 vols. (1835; New York: D. Appleton, 1899), and Harriet Martineau, *Society in America* (1837; Garden City, N.Y.: Doubleday, 1962). Social historians have questioned the "egalitarian myth" of antebellum America perpetuated by Tocqueville and others. For a particularly critical view of Tocqueville's claims concerning the equal distribution of wealth during the antebellum era, see Edward Pessen, "The Egalitarian Myth and American Social Reality: Wealth, Mobility, and Equality in the 'Era of the Common Man' " (*American Historical Review* 76 [October 1971]: 989–1034), and Pessen, *Riches, Class, and Power before the Civil War* (Lexington, Mass.: D. C. Heath, 1973), though Pessen focuses mainly on the inequality in urban areas. In the past two decades, numerous studies analyzing the distribution of wealth in rural areas of the antebellum North have tended to support Tocqueville's view that the region was one of relative equality. These studies include Lee Soltow, *Men and Wealth in the United States, 1850–1870* (New Haven: Yale University Press, 1975); Soltow, "Tocqueville's View of the Northwest in 1835: Ohio a Generation after Settlement," in *Essays on the Economy of the Old Northwest*, edited by David C. Klingaman and Richard K. Vedder (Athens: Ohio University Press, 1987); Peter Lindert, *Fertility and Scarcity in America* (Princeton: Princeton University Press, 1978); and Jeremy Atack and Fred Bateman, *To Their Own Soil: Agriculture in the Antebellum North* (Ames: Iowa State University Press, 1987).

Eighteenth- and nineteenth-century reports on the relationship between population density and fertility rates in general and the experience of America in particular can be found as early as Adam Smith, *An Inquiry into the Nature and Causes of the Wealth of Nations*, 2 vols. (1776; Chicago: University of Chicago Press, 1976). The seminal work on population density and economic

147

growth is Thomas Robert Malthus, *An Essay on the Principle of Population and a Summary View of the Principle of Population* (1798; Baltimore: Penguin, 1970). Nineteenth-century American writers who identified the density-fertility relationship include Ezra Seaman, *Essay on the Progress of Nations* (New York: C. W. Benedict, 1843), and George Tucker, *Progress of the United States in Population and Wealth in Fifty Years* (1855; New York: Augustus M. Kelly, 1964). The empirical evidence in these studies is crude by current standards, and some of the theories have not stood up well over time; nonetheless, they show that contemporaries recognized the demographic change taking place in eighteenth- and nineteenth-century America and understood that the change was related to economic variables.

Empirical studies illustrating the fertility behavior of nineteenth-century populations in developed countries in general and the rural United States in particular make up a vast body of literature. A few of the most important studies focusing on international trends are John C. Caldwell, *Theory of Fertility Decline* (London: Academic Press, 1982); Ansley J. Coale and Susan Cotts Watkins, eds., *Decline of Fertility in Europe* (Princeton: Princeton University Press, 1986); Ansley Coale, "The Demographic Transition," in *Proceedings of the International Population Conference, Liege*, vol. 1 (Liege: IUSSP, 1973); Coale and E. M. Hoover, *Population Growth and Development in Low Income Countries* (Princeton: Princeton University Press, 1958); Frank W. Notestein, "Population—The Long View," in *Food for the World*, edited by Theodore W. Schultz (Chicago: University of Chicago Press, 1945); Notestein, "Economic Problems of Population Change," in *Proceedings of the Eighth International Conference of Agricultural Economists, 1953* (London: Oxford University Press, 1953); George J. Stolnitz, "The Demographic Transition: From High to Low Birth Rates and Death Rates," in *Population: The Vital Revolution*, edited by Ronald Freedman (New York: Anchor, 1964); and Etienne van de Walle and John Knodel, "Europe's Fertility Transition: New Evidence and Lessons for Today's Developing World" (*Population Bulletin* 34 [1980]: 3–43).

Numerous volumes analyzed the demographic history of the United States. Among these are Ansley Coale and Melvin Zelnick, *New Estimates of Fertility and Population in the United States* (Princeton: Princeton University Press, 1973); Colin Foster and G. S. L. Tucker, *Economic Opportunity and White American Fertility Ratios, 1800–1860* (New Haven: Yale University Press, 1972); Wilson H. Grabill, Clyde V. Kiser, and Pascal K. Whelpton, *The Fertility of American Women* (New York: John Wiley and Sons, 1958); Lindert, *Fertility and Scarcity in America*; Conrad Taeuber and Irene B. Taeuber, *The Changing Population of the United States* (New York: John Wiley and Sons, 1958); Warren S. Thompson and P. K. Whelpton, *Population Trends in the United States* (New York: McGraw-Hill, 1933); and Yasukichi Yasuba, *Birth Rates of the White Population in the United States* (Baltimore: Johns Hopkins University Press, 1961).

Many studies identifying the Malthusian relationship between land scarcity or rural economic stress and fertility behavior in antebellum America can be found, including Atack and Bateman, *To Their Own Soil*; Wendell H. Bash,

"Differential Fertility in Madison County, New York, 1865" (*Millbank Memorial Fund Quarterly* 33 [April 1955]: 161–186) and Bash, "Changing Birth Rates in Developing America: New York State, 1840–1875" (*Millbank Memorial Fund Quarterly* 41 [April 1963]: 161–182). The seminal work on the targeted bequest hypothesis is that of Richard A. Easterlin, "Does Human Fertility Adjust to Environment?" (*American Economic Review* 61 [May 1971]: 399–407); see also Easterlin, "Relative Economic Status and the American Fertility Swing," in *Family Problems and Prospects*, edited by E. B. Sheldon (Philadelphia: Lippincott, 1973); Easterlin, "Population Change and Farm Settlement in the Northern United States" (*Journal of Economic History* 37 [March 1976]: 45–75; Allan G. Bogue, "Comment on 'Population Change and Farm Settlement in the Northern United States' " (*Journal of Economic History*) 37 [March 1976]: 76–81); Richard A. Easterlin, "Factors in the Decline of Farm Family Fertility in the United States: Some Preliminary Results" (*Journal of American History* 63 [December 1976]: 600–614); and Easterlin, George Alter, and Gretchen Condran, "Farms and Farm Families in Old and New Areas: The Northern States in 1860," in *Family and Population in Nineteenth Century America*, edited by Tamara Hareven and Maris Vinoskis (Princeton: Princeton University Press, 1976).

Other work along the same lines includes Donald R. Leet, "Human Fertility and Agricultural Opportunities in Ohio Counties: From Frontier to Maturity, 1810–60," in *Essays in Nineteenth Century Economic History: The Old Northwest,* edited by David C. Klingaman and Richard K. Vedder (Athens: Ohio University Press, 1976); Leet, "The Determinants of the Fertility Transition in Antebellum Ohio" (*Journal of Economic History* 36 [June 1976]: 359–78); Morton Schapiro, *Filling Up America: An Economic-Demographic Model of Population Growth and Distribution in the Nineteenth Century United States* (Greenwich, Conn.: JAI Press, 1986); and Schapiro, "Land Availability and Fertility in the United States, 1760–1870" (*Journal of Economic History* 42 [September 1982]: 577–600).

Several studies emphasize other theories of fertility behavior, including the importance of strategic bequests and changes in the direction of intergenerational transfers in fertility decline. These include Gary S. Becker, "An Economic Analysis of Fertility," in *Demographics and Economic Change in Developed Countries* (Princeton: Princeton University Press, 1960), and reprinted in *The Economic Approach to Human Behavior* (Chicago: University of Chicago Press, 1976); Gary S. Becker. and Robert J. Barro, "A Reformulation of the Economic Theory of Fertility," paper prepared for Conference on Causes and Consequences of Non-Replacement Fertility, Hoover Institute, 1985; Gary S. Becker and Nigel Tomes, "Child Endowments and the Quantity and Quality of Children" (*Journal of Political Economy* 84 [July 1984]: pt. 2, S143–S162); B. Douglas Bernheim, Andrei Shleifer, and Lawrence Summers, "The Strategic Bequest Motive" (*Journal of Political Economy* 93 [November 1985]: 1045–76); David Bevan and Joseph Stiglitz, "Intergenerational Transfers and Inequality" (*Greek Economic Review* 1 [April 1979]: 8–26); Paul A. David and William A. Sundstrom, "Bargains, Bequests, and Births," Stanford Project on the History of Fertility Control, 1984; Roger L. Ransom and Richard Sutch,

"Did Rising Out Migration Cause Fertility to Decline in AnteBellum New England?" Cal-Tech Social Science Working Paper 610, 1986; Ransom and Sutch, "Babies or Bank Accounts? Two Strategies for a More Secure Old Age," University of California Project on the History of Saving, working paper, 1987; and William A. Sundstrom and Paul A. David, "Old-Age Security Motives, Labor Markets, and Farm Family Fertility in Antebellum America" (*Explorations in Economic History* 25 [April 1988]: 164–97).

Chapter 2
The Value of Output and the Division of Labor on the Family Farm

Several important volumes analyzing a multitude of topics on rural life in the antebellum North have been compiled over the years. The best recent empirical study of both the economic and demographic aspects of northern agriculture is Jeremy Atack and Fred Bateman, *To Their Own Soil: Agriculture in the AnteBellum North* (Ames: Iowa State University Press, 1987). Anyone seeking a quantitative survey of rural economic life in the antebellum North would do well to begin with that volume.

Other earlier studies include six classics, which no serious student of the topic can ignore. They are Percy Bidwell and John Falconer, *History of Agriculture in the Northern United States, 1620–1860* (Washington, D.C.: Carnegie Institute, 1925); Allan G. Bogue, *From Prairie to Corn Belt: Farming on the Illinois and Iowa Prairie* (Chicago: University of Chicago Press, 1963); Clarence H. Danhof, *Change in Agriculture: The Northern United States, 1820–1870* (Cambridge: Harvard University Press, 1969); Paul Wallace Gates, *The Farmer's Age, 1815–1860* (New York: Holt, Rinehart, and Winston, 1960); Gates, *Landlords and Tenants on the Prairie Frontier* (Ithaca: Cornell University Press, 1973); and Robert P. Swierenga, *Pioneers and Profits: Land Speculation on the Iowa Frontier* (Ames: Iowa State University Press, 1968).

Two fine volumes of collected essays on the economy of the Old Northwest are David C. Klingaman and Richard K. Vedder, eds., *Essays in Nineteenth Century Economic History: The Old Northwest* (Athens: Ohio University Press, 1975), and Klingaman and Vedder, eds., *Essays on the Economy of the Old Northwest* (Athens: Ohio University Press, 1987). As with most volumes of papers by many authors, the coverage in these two is sometimes idiosyncratic, but for quantitative papers on the Old Northwest they are hard to beat. For an excellent set of papers discussing the nature of northern agriculture in relation to the South, Europe, and the industrial sector, see William N. Parker's essays, in *Europe, America, and the Wider World: Vol. 2, America and the Wider World* (Cambridge: Cambridge University Press, 1991). No economic historian is more in touch with "the whole man" who inhabited the northern countryside than Parker.

Anyone interested in the study of nineteenth-century farm labor must read David Schob, *Hired Hands and Plowboys: Farm Labor in the Midwest, 1815–1860* (Urbana: University of Illinois Press, 1975). No volume provides a more comprehensive look at the day-to-day tasks and compensation of farm labor than this excellent book, which contains countless examples of narrative evidence describing the allocation and wages of household labor. Another valuable source of narrative evidence concerning daily life on a nineteenth-century northern farm is Laura Ingalls Wilder's "Little House" series, in particular, *Farmer Boy* (New York: Harper and Row, 1971) and *Little House in the Big Woods* (New York: Harper and Row, 1971). These books provide splendid eyewitness descriptions of everything from churning butter and making lard to threshing grain and harvesting potatoes.

The data employed for most of the empirical analysis come from the matched sample of more than 20,000 households from the 1860 census of population and agriculture, constructed by Fred Bateman and James Foust. Descriptions of the sample can be found in Atack and Bateman, *To Their Own Soil*; Bateman and Foust, "A Sample of Rural Households Selected from the 1860 Manuscript Censuses" (*Agricultural History* 48 [Winter 1974]: 75–93); and Bateman and Foust, "*Agricultural and Demographic Records of 21,118 Rural Households Selected from the 1860 Manuscript Censuses*," Magnetic tape, Indiana University, 1974, financed by the National Science Foundation under Grant AS-27143, user's guide.

The description of the mechanization of grain farming and the subsequent changes in the economic roles of women and children owes much to the classic work by Leo Rogin, *The Introduction of Farm Machinery* (Berkeley: University of California Press, 1931). More recent studies on mechanization include Atack and Bateman, *To Their Own Soil*; Paul A. David, "The Mechanization of Reaping in the Ante-bellum Midwest," in *Industrialization in Two Systems*, edited by H. Rosovsky (New York: John Wiley and Sons, 1966); Alan L. Olmstead, "The Mechanization of Reaping and Mowing in American Agriculture" (*Journal of Economic History* 35 [June 1975]: 327–52); and R. Douglas Hurt, *American Farm Tools: From Hand-Power to Steam-Power* (Manhattan, Kans.: Sunflower University Press, 1982).

Information on the size of the antebellum labor force can be found in Stanley Lebergott, *Manpower in Economic Growth* (New York: McGraw-Hill, 1964), and Eleanor von Ende and Thomas Weiss, "Labor Force Changes in the Old Northwest," in *Essays on the Economy of the Old Northwest*, edited by David C. Klingaman and Richard K. Vedder (Athens: Ohio University Press, 1987). The controversy on the productivity of American agricultural labor relative to European labor comes from a debate between Gregory Clark and John Komlos. See Gregory Clark, "Productivity Growth Without Technical Change in European Agriculture Before 1850" (*Journal of Economic History* 47 [June 1987]: 419–32); John Komlos, "Agricultural Productivity in America and Eastern Europe: A Comment" (*Journal of Economic History* 48 [September 1988]: 655–64); and Gregory Clark, "Productivity Growth Without Technical Change in European Agriculture: Reply to Komlos" (*Journal of Economic History* 49 [December 1989]: 979–91). Data comparing yields of American and European farms can be found in Atack and Bateman, *To Their Own Soil*; B. H. Slicher van Bath, *Agrarian History of Western Europe: A.D. 500–1850* (London: Arnold, 1963); and Komlos, "Agricultural Productivity."

Converting the multitude of crops and other types of output produced on antebellum farms into corn equivalents required the energy conversion factors found in F. B. Morrison, *Feeds and Feeding* (Ithaca, New York: Morrison, 1955), and United Nations Food and Agriculture Organization, *Technical Conversion Factors for Agricultural Commodities* (Rome: F.A.O., 1960). The following studies contain estimates of the productivity and consumption by members of the household relative to adult males, and/or estimates of the value of children: U.S. Bureau of Labor Statistics, "Estimating Equivalent Incomes or Budget Costs by Family Types" (*Monthly Labor Review* 83 [November 1960]: 1197–1202); Mead T. Cain, "The Economic Activities of Children in a Village in Bangladesh" (*Population Development Review* 3 [1977]: 201–27); Frank Lorimer, "The Economics of Family Formation under Different Conditions," in *World Population Conference*, vol. 2 (New York: United Nations Press, 1965); Eva Mueller, "The Economic Value of Children in Peasant Agriculture," in *Population and Development*, edited by Ronald Ridker (Baltimore: Johns Hopkins University Press, 1976); S. J. Prais and H. S. Houthakker, *The Analysis of Family Budgets* (New York: Cambridge University Press, 1955); J. R. N. Stone, *The Measurement of Consumer's Expenditure and Behavior in the United Kingdom, 1920–1938*, vol. 1 (Cambridge: Cambridge University Press, 1954); C. H. Wold, *Demand Analysis* (New York: John Wiley and Sons, 1953); and Robert Woodbury, "Economic Consumption Scales and Their Uses" (*Journal of the American Statistical Association* 32 [1944]: 445–68).

Estimating the components of gross revenue required data and other information from many sources. For the returns to land, see Stanley Lebergott, "The Demand for Land: The U.S., 1820–1860" (*Journal of Economic History* 45 [June 1985]: 181–212); Lebergott, " 'O Pioneers': Land Speculation and the Growth of the Midwest," edited by David C. Klingaman and Richard K. Vedder (Athens: Ohio University Press, 1987); and Peter Lindert, "Long-Run Trends in American Farm Land Values" (*Agricultural History* 62 [Summer 1988]: 45–85). For the estimation of dairy and poultry products, see Fred Bateman, "Improvement in American Dairy Farming 1850–1910: A Quantitative Analysis" (*Journal of Economic History* 28 [June 1968]: 255–73), and F. Strauss and L. H. Bean, "Gross Farm Income and Indices of Farm Production and Prices in the United States, 1869–1937," *USDA technical bulletin 703* (Washington, D.C.: USDA, 1940).

Other U.S. government publications from which data were drawn include Census Office, Eighth Census, *Agriculture in the United States in 1860* (Washington, D.C.: Government Printing Office, 1864); Census Office, Tenth Census, *Report upon the Statistics of Agriculture Compiled from Returns Received at the Tenth Census* (Washington, D.C.: Government Printing Office, 1883); Census Office, Fifteenth Census, *Agriculture Volume II, Part 1—The Northern States* (Washington, D.C.: Government Printing Office, 1932); Census Office, Sixteenth Census, *Agriculture Volume II, Parts 1–3* (Washington, D.C.: Government Printing Office, 1942); Commerce Department, *Historical Statistics of the U.S., Colonial Times to 1970* (Washington, D.C.: Government Printing Office, 1975); Department of Agriculture, *Farm Wage Rates, Farm Employment, and Related Data* (Washington, D.C.: Bureau of Agricultural Economics, 1943); and Patent Office, *Report of the Commissioner of Patents, Part II, Agriculture* (Washington, D.C.: Government Printing Office, 1850–57).

For a detailed discussion of most of the sources of information used for the calculation of gross farm revenue and a summary of the information from each source, see Lee A. Craig, "Farm Output, Productivity, and Fertility Decline in the Antebellum Northern United States," dissertation, Indiana University, 1989.

Chapter 3
The Allocation of Farm Labor and the Life Cycle
of the Household

Several studies touching on aging and the intergenerational transfer of wealth in colonial and antebellum America have been written in the past two decades. They include David Hackett Fischer, *Growing Old in America* (New York: Oxford University Press, 1977); Philip J. Greven, Jr., *Four Generations: Population, Land, and Family in Colonial Andover Massachusetts* (Ithaca: Cornell University Press, 1970); Carole Haber, *Beyond Sixty-Five: The Dilemma of Old Age in America's Past* (Cambridge: Cambridge University Press, 1983); and Carole Shammas, Marylynn Salmon, and Michel Dahlin, *Inheritance in America from Colonial Times to the Present* (New Brunswick, N.J.: Rutgers University Press, 1987).

On the definition of the life cycle of the individual versus that of the family or household and on the problem created by the use of cross-sectional data, see Lutz Berkner, "The Stem Family and the Developmental Cycle of the Peasant Household" (*American Historical Review* 77 [April 1972]: 398–412); Berkner, "The Use and Misuse of Census Data for the Historical Analysis of Family Structure" (*Journal of Interdisciplinary History* 5 [Spring 1975]: 721–38); and Berkner, "Household Arithmetic: A Note" (*Journal of Family History* 2 [Spring 1977]: 159–163).

The discussion of the potentially conflicting effects on the allocation household labor resulting from the composition of the family and the location of the farm owes much to the underappreciated volume by A. V. Chayanov, *The Theory of the Peasant Economy*, edited by Daniel Thorner, Basile Kerblay, and R. E. F. Smith (Homewood, Ill.: Irwin, 1966). Although much of the discussion and methodology employed by Chayanov may seem unfamiliar and idiosyncratic to contemporary neoclassical economists, his insights into the structure of the peasant household and its potential for both change and intransigence in relation to external forces are invaluable to anyone who studies the economics of rural life.

Other work on the allocation of labor and crop mix in this and other settings includes Heywood Fleisig, "Slavery, the Supply of Agricultural Labor, and the Industrialization of the South" (*Journal of Economic History* 36 [September 1976]: 573–97); Gavin Wright, *The Political Economy of the Cotton South* (New York: W. W. Norton, 1978); and William N. Parker, "Agriculture," in *American Economic Growth*, edited by Lance Davis, Richard Easterlin, William Parker, et al. (New York: Harper and Row, 1972).

Chapter 4
The Economic Value of Women and Children
in Northern Agriculture

I have refererred to many other studies on the economy of nineteenth-century America in order to compare my estimates of the value of household labor against those of others. These include, Fred Bateman and Jeremy Atack, "The Profitability of Northern Agriculture in 1860" (*Research in Economic History* 4 [1979]: 345–63); Alfred H. Conrad and John C. Meyer, "The Economics of Slavery in the Antebellum South" (*Journal of Political Economy* 66 [April 1958]: 95–122); Robert Fogel and Stanley Engerman, *Time on the Cross* (Boston: University Press of America, 1974); Claudia Goldin and Kenneth Sokoloff, "Women, Children, and Industrialization in the Early Republic" (*Journal of Economic History* 42 [December 1982]: 741–74); and Goldin and Sokoloff, "The Relative Productivity Hypothesis of Industrialization" (*Quarterly Journal of Economics* 69 [August 1984]: 3, 461–88).

Numerous studies have been conducted estimating aggregate production functions. Among these are E. R. Berndt and L. R. Christensen, "Testing for the Existence of a Consistent Aggregate Index of Labor Inputs" (*American Economic Review* 60 [June 1974]: 391–404); Christensen, D. W. Jorgenson, and L. J. Lau, "Transcendental Logarithmic Production Frontiers" (*Review of Economics and Statistics* 60 [January 1973]: 28–45); and Elizabeth B. Field, "The Relative Efficiency of Slavery Revisited: A Translog Production Function Approach" (*American Economic Review* 78 [June 1988]: 543–49). For a discussion of the problems encountered in the estimation in table 4.2 and suggested remedies, see Henri Theil, *Principles of Econometrics* (New York: John Wiley and Sons, 1971).

Estimates of the productivity of household labor can be found in Lee A. Craig, "The Value of Household Labor in Antebellum Northern Agriculture" (*Journal of Economic History* 51 [March 1991]: 67–82); and Craig, "Farm Output, Productivity, and Fertility Decline in the Antebellum Northern United States," dissertation Indiana University, 1989. Comparisons between the productivity of male and female labor in different sectors and regions of the antebellum era can be found in Lee A. Craig and Elizabeth Field-Hendrey, "Industrialization and the Earnings Gap" (*Explorations in Economic History* 30 [Spring 1993]: 60–80.

Models of the household that either directly or indirectly relate to fertility behavior include the following: Gary S. Becker, "A Theory of the Allocation of Time" (*Economic Journal* 75 [1965]: 493–517), reprinted in Becker, *The Economic Approach to Human Behavior* (Chicago: University of Chicago Press, 1976); Becker, "On the Interaction Between the Quantity and Quality of Children" (*Journal of Political Economy* 81 [April 1973]: 2, pt. 2, S279–S288), reprinted in Becker, *Economic Approach to Human Behavior*; Peter Lindert, *Fertility and Scarcity in America* (Princeton: Princeton University Press, 1978); Robert A. Pollack, "A Transaction Cost Approach to Families and Households" (*Journal of Economic Literature* 23 [June 1985]: 581–608); Robert Repetto, "Direct Economic Costs and Value of Children," in *Popu-*

lation and Development, edited by Ronald Ridker (Baltimore: Johns Hopkins University Press, 1976); Mark R. Rosenzweig, "The Demand for Children in Farm Households" (*Journal of Political Economy* 85 [February 1977]: 123–46); and Robert J. Willis, "A New Approach to the Economic Theory of Fertility Behavior" (*Journal of Political Economy* 81 [April 1973]: pt. 2, S14–S64).

Index

157

To Sow One Acre More

Designed by Ann Walston

Composed by JDL Composition Services
in Times Roman

Printed by The Maple Press Company
on 50-lb. MV Eggshell Cream